BREAKING THROUGH THE STAINED GLASS CEILING

Shattering Myths and Empowering Women for

Leadership in the Church

Beth Jones

TABLE OF CONTENTS

DEDICATION

To my wonderful husband Jeff; I am so glad the Lord called us to "magnify His name together"—it's been the adventure of a lifetime and there's no one I'd rather be doing life with! You are the funniest and most selfless, servant-hearted person I know. You have always believed in me, encouraged me and made a way for me—thank you. I love you dearly!

To our daughters Meghan and Annie, and our sons Luke and Eric; I have no greater joy than in being your mom and watching you all grow into the amazing people God has created you to be. Thank you for being the best, for making me laugh, for "the cool club mocking" and for being "good PKs!" I love you forever!

To my mom, Carol Barker; you were a single mom raising us four girls when it wasn't easy, popular or commonplace. Thank you for setting the bar high and showing us how to survive and thrive. We have so many fun memories of our little "sorority" with you at the helm. Love you mom!

To my younger sisters, Rhonda, Kelly and Michelle; everything I learned about leadership, influence and persuasive speech, I first learned from leading you! What a blast it was to grow up with all of you. I am so proud of the godly women, wives, moms and amazing leaders all of you have become. Love you!

To Valley Family Church; what a journey we have been on!

Together, we've seen God help thousands of people "get it." Thank you for allowing me to serve as the "mom of the house" and for receiving me as a pastor, leader and teacher with such open arms and hearts. Love you all!

To the next generation of women leaders; you were in my heart as I wrote this book—especially my daughters—Meghan Hock and Annie Jones, and the young ninja's who assist us and run Jeff and Beth Jones Ministries—Kelsey Wilson, Alexa Wolfe, Amanda Harrison and Tara Hoult, and my nieces—Erica Giesow, Chelsea Groenewegen, Morgan Albert, Hannah Adams and Tiffany Rogers. To every young girl out there who dreams of teaching, preaching, leading, pastoring and changing the world—whether you work with your husband or you're going solo—God has called you for such a time as this, break through that glass! I am cheering you on!

ENDORSEMENTS

I love Pastor Beth Jones' heart to see women in the church realize their voice & reach their full potential!

Lisa Bevere
Best-Selling Author/Minister
Messenger International

Women have always been important in my life. I've been surrounded by them—my mother, my siblings were sisters, my wife, my two kids are both women, my two grandbabies are, yes you guessed it, women! Even my dog was a woman. What Pastor Beth Jones describes in her book *Breaking Through the Stained Glass Ceiling: Shattering Myths and Empowering Women for Leadership in the Church* was always assumed by me and now affirmed with biblical and pragmatic truths. Beth Jones will take you on her and other women's journeys of wrestling, accepting and flourishing in what God intended them to be—you'll love it.

Dr. Samuel R. Chand
Leadership Consultant
Author, *Cracking Your Church's Culture Code*

In this book, Beth Jones presents a balanced and biblical approach to embracing women in ministry.

Steve Kelly
Senior Pastor, Wave Church
Virginia Beach, Virginia

A clarion call to the Church for the 21st Century and beyond! *Breaking Through the Stained Glass Ceiling* is biblically sound with both historical and contemporary models of God's call to women in ministry at all levels of His Church. Both energy and honesty radiate from the writings. A must-read for all women and men who care about a broken world that Christ longs to redeem.

Jo Anne Lyon
General Superintendent
The Wesleyan Church

Beth presents both a compelling and undeniable case that women are, in fact, called in every arena of ministry/culture to take God's message to the world. Myths are shattered as Beth provides clear biblical and historical explanations for each and every controversial scripture on the subject of women in ministry. A must-read for all men and women who desire to KNOW the truth on this subject!

Nancy Alcorn
Founder and President
Mercy Ministries

Beth Jones nails it again! I served as a pastor for over 30 years, and in all those years I've never seen such a simple, Scriptural, and well-researched writing on the subject of women in the ministry. Beth masterfully dispels the so-called biblical "contradictions" and myths concerning women pastors and ministers in the Church. It's time to stop the arguing and nit-picking and get on with the Kingdom work! Ladies, get ready to break through the stained glass ceiling.

Dave Williams
Author, *Pacesetting Leadership*
Lansing, Michigan

In every society there are voices that must be heard. Beth Jones is one of those voices for our generation. Beth, because of the journey she has taken, the challenges she has faced, and the faith she has lived; has written a book, which for me is a must-read. Her book begins to elevate the possibilities and speak to the heart of issues which are too often avoided. I want to say personally as a pastor of 37 years, there's nothing that can replace the wisdom of godly ladies like Beth. I encourage you to learn and grow from this outstanding leader and minister. The question, "Can ladies teach men?" The answer is simple: "Absolutely." The bigger question is, "Will men listen?" That question really requires another book.

Gerald Brooks, DD
Senior Pastor, Grace Outreach Center
Plano, Texas

My husband Philip and I have been pastoring Oasis Church together for 30 years. We love that we get to build God's house together. We believe that just like a two-parent home is the best way to raise a child, a church with both a 'mom' and a 'dad' is the best way to raise a spiritual family. In her book *Breaking Through the Stained Glass Ceiling*, Beth Jones shares her story as a woman co-pastoring alongside her husband and all the joys and challenges that come with that role. She tackles some of the hard questions about women in leadership and confronts some old thought patterns. You will laugh and learn! This is a great book...and a must-read for any woman in ministry and any woman seeking to fulfill her purpose in God!

Holly Wagner
Pastor, Oasis Church
Founder, GodChicks
Los Angeles, California

Beth Jones has tackled a topic that begs to be tackled in the church today. Her heart has been poured onto every page; and with humor, directness and her own amazingly clear style, Beth lays a foundation on which women can build key positions in ministry leadership. This book isn't just about debating for the role of women in the church. It's all about empowering people everywhere to understand the potential God has given to women to lead out as we advance His kingdom!

Lisa Young
Wife of Pastor Ed Young, Fellowship Church
Author, *The Creative Marriage* and *The Marriage Mirror*
Founder, Flavour: Women Becoming World Changers
Grapevine, Texas

Breaking Through the Stained Glass Ceiling is an excellent book that I am pleased to heartily recommend. Beth Jones does a great job of covering what has often been considered controversial material from different and necessary perspectives—subjectively and objectively, theologically, historically, and culturally. I believe many people will have their own perspectives wonderfully broadened and that many will find great liberty and empowerment through what Beth has written. I am 100% behind this work.

Tony Cooke
Author, *Your Place on God's Dream Team* and *In Search of Timothy*
Tulsa, Oklahoma

Breaking Through the Stained Glass Ceiling will change your thinking on the purpose of women in ministry. Beth Jones' transparency and knowledge on this important subject demonstrates God's heart relating to women. Get out there girls and live the life God intended for you!

Sandy Scheer
Co-Pastor, Guts Church
Tulsa, Oklahoma

Breaking Through the Stained Glass Ceiling is a brilliant, encouraging, uplifting and much needed book. As you read through each chapter you will be amazed and built up by the wisdom Beth shares. Be ready to be captivated; and be challenged to stay the course in becoming the woman God has called you to be.

Wendy Treat
Pastor, Christian Faith Center
Author, *Shoes Wisely* and *Take a God Look at Yourself*
Federal Way, Washington

What an encouragement it was to read Beth Jones' book – *Breaking Through the Stained Glass Ceiling*. Beth thoughtfully and carefully examined scriptures regarding the role of women as prophets, preachers and teachers while overlaying the cultural context of the times. The result is a complex and yet clear message that God indeed planned always for women to serve alongside men in these important life roles. I encourage men and women to read and explore this important book. Together we can go so much farther and faster to accomplish the Great Commission Jesus gave us if we will only empower and support women to serve alongside men.

Linda Stanley
Vice-President & Team Leader, Leadership Network
Dallas, Texas

There is a Chinese saying about one of the qualities of a pioneer as someone who is willing to "eat the crab" without being fearful of its pincer. Beth has dealt with this sensitive issue biblically and boldly in order to set women free to serve in a spiritual leadership capacity. I am confident that you will be greatly blessed!

Daniel Ho
Senior Pastor, International Church of Shanghai
Shanghai, China

Breaking Through the Stained Glass Ceiling answers questions commonly heard regarding a woman in ministry. Can I teach men? Who was Paul talking about? Does this scripture apply to me? How can I be a wife who honors her husband and fulfill my calling as a preacher or teacher? Am I only ever destined to teach women? Beth does a superb job of simplifying and explaining what seems to be a contradiction in Scripture to show how women have always been a part of God's original plan to help and partner with God and man to accomplish His will on earth.

Patsy Cameneti
Co-Director, Rhema Australia
Author, *For Such a Time as This*
Brisbane, Australia

For decades Beth Jones, cofounder of Valley Family Church, has provided phenomenal, visionary leadership. Her latest book, *Breaking Through The Stained Glass Ceiling,* is a must-read in the 21st Century Global Church. Beth focuses a powerful, biblical lens on the present and future leadership roles of women in ministry worldwide. I highly recommend every Christian leader to read, study and apply the principles and practices taught within its pages.

James O. Davis
Cofounder, Billion Souls Network
Author, *Making Your Net Work*
Greater Orlando, Florida

Thank God, Beth Jones is shattering those tired-old misconceptions that have limited the role of women in the church. By rightly dividing the Word, she reveals the truth contained in the "spirit" and not the "letter" of the law. We would do well to follow the lead of Jesus, the Great CEO, who entrusted the work and teaching of His ministry to men and women alike. Even as a trained and powerful soldier is submissive to his or her rank, we women can be bold and effective in our calling and still remain balanced. Look out! Shards of glass are flying now! A fearless army of intelligent, passionate, Spirit-filled gals is *Breaking Through the Stained Glass Ceiling* and spreading the Gospel with confidence! It's the devil's worst nightmare! Go, you preacher girls! Stay true to your gifts and calling. It's okay...you may be the only one in high-heels!!!

Nicole Crank
Co-Pastor, Faith Church
St. Louis, Missouri

Beth Jones is an incredible example to men and women in this day and age. She naturally leads and runs alongside her husband in her God-given lane without striving. She has wrestled with this subject personally and walks in great and humble revelation. She tackles the tough questions and controversial verses we've all heard and brings a refreshing, insightful and intelligent response to tricky questions we all face in this season as The church on the earth. I would strongly encourage you to read this book for yourself, wrestle with these questions that we're all faced with, and get revelation on this vital subject.

Andi Andrew
Lead Pastor, Liberty Church NYC
New York, New York

I picked this book up to scan it and literally could not put it down – it's so well written and the content is completely captivating. It's not only biblically accurate, but it's full of stories and encouragement from the lives of real women who are serving God with all their hearts. Every woman needs to read this book – this is your time! Work!

Karen Jensen Salisbury
Speaker & Author, *Why God Why?*
Minneapolis, Minnesota

The lingering debate taking place within the walls of the church over women being qualified to lead has consumed time and energy better spent outside the walls of the church. It is time that we explore the heart of truth concerning this matter and focus our energy on becoming a collective army marching in agreement with His Word! To this end, Beth Jones has diligently searched the Scriptures, holding fast to the integrity of truth, and has courageously presented her findings here. *Breaking Through the Stained Glass Ceiling* allows us to explore a path of clarity, which will enable the Church to step into the fullness of empowerment and the fullness of our collective mandate.

Dennis & Colleen Rouse
Pastors, Victory World Church
Atlanta, Georgia

Breaking Through the Stained Glass Ceiling shatters centuries of religious beliefs and myths that have kept women from connecting to their God-given purpose. Written with humor and sharing from personal experience Beth gives a balanced look into the strength that emerges when men and women are empowered to work together as a team to build the church. Beth's passion to see generations of women rise up and take their place will encourage you to discover your value, purpose and the amazing gifts you have to offer the world around you.

Donna Pisani
Co-Lead Pastor, Capital City Church
Washington, DC

We are called to invade culture with excellence and as usual, Beth uses her gift to do just that. Her straightforward writing puts you in the thick of it. Not to be missed.

Keith & Mary Hudson
Keith Hudson Ministries

I can't see the pages anymore and the world has gone white and still through the tears streaming down my face as the Holy Spirit ministers to my heart. Sitting in seat 17C on my way to Rio De Janeiro, Brazil, I look around to see if anyone notices, then I realize I don't care. God has just spoken to me ~ *Breaking Through the Stained Glass Ceiling* breaks the chains and blows the ceiling off the stained glass boxes women have been put in for centuries. Beth Jones rightly divides the scriptures and reminds us all that God gave us permission to fulfill the Great Commission Jesus assigned us to begin with! I would summarize it this way, "Your limitations are only real if you believe them." Choose to go up and out of your Stained Glass Ceiling with Beth and experience the freedom and joy of serving the Lord Jesus Christ with the Power of the Holy Spirit!

Rhonda Rogers
Co-Pastor Rhema Bible Church & Co-Director, Rhema Mexico
Mexico City, Mexico

I would encourage any woman who has a calling into ministry to read this timely book, *Breaking Through the Stained Glass Ceiling.* Beth has written a thorough, yet easy to read teaching of the biblical role of women in the church. I appreciate the personal examples she shares of her obedience to the call of God, no matter what the criticism, and the fruit of lives that have been impacted for eternity. This book highlights godly women who have paved the way so that other generations of women can walk in greater freedom and faith in serving God. I believe as you read this book, you will be encouraged and inspired to boldly walk in the purpose God has for your life.

Sarah Wehrli
Co-Pastor, Victory Orlando
Author, *Awake: Rise to Your Divine Assignment*
Orlando, Florida

Beth Jones is one of my favorite Bible teachers! Her commitment to truth, scholarship and engaging narrative has thrilled my heart for years. Her journalistic gifts have enriched all of Christianity time and time again. In *Breaking Through the Stained Glass Ceiling*, Beth has done an incredible job addressing the question of women in leadership within the church. This book doesn't gloss over the "hard texts" but takes you on a journey of fresh discovery and freedom. Its thought-provoking defense of truth is very compelling. Nobody articulates and clarifies quite like the unique gifts God has given Beth Jones. I am so excited for readers to experience the ministerial beauty that women have in Christ. Anyone stuck in a religious fog about women leading/teaching MUST make this a priority read; it will serve as a gift they give to themselves. I highly recommend this great work!

Patrick Norris
Pastor, LifePointe Church
Overland Park, Kansas

ACKNOWLEDGMENTS

I am thankful for the countless women—those known and unknown by men, but certainly known by heaven—who pioneered and blazed a gospel trail over the years along with the wonderful men who embraced and encouraged them to do so. Some I have just read about and a few I have had the pleasure of getting to know. Thank you to all the women who have gone before us in answering His call. Your legacy lives on in many generations of women who are breaking through the stained glass ceiling to impact this world for Jesus Christ.

I especially want to thank the women who have contributed their stories and words of wisdom in the "Women Leaders in the Church" profiles highlighted throughout the book as well as each woman who endorsed this project. I respect and admire you all greatly. Thank you Dodie Osteen, Lisa Osteen Comes, Tamara Osteen Graff, April Osteen Simons, Jennifer Osteen, Victoria Osteen, Sandy Scheer, Lisa Young, Wendy Treat, Holly Wagner, Colleen Rouse, Sarah Wehrli, Nicole Crank and Andi Andrew. Thank you Lisa Bevere, JoAnn Lyon, Nancy Alcorn, Linda Stanley, Patsy Cameneti, Karen Jensen Salisbury, Donna Pisani, Mary Hudson and Rhonda Rogers.

I want to honor Dave Williams, one of my first pastors and a great encourager. You were the first person to invite me to speak from a pulpit, in a church on a Wednesday night to a crowd of men and women at Mount Hope Assembly. For many, it was just another Wednesday night, for me, it was a marked moment. Thank you—through that experience I got a taste of what God had in store for me—and Jeff and I started dating on that very night!

Pastor Ken and Lynette Hagin; you were the first to recognize Jeff and I as a husband/wife ministry team when you invited us to lead the singles School of the Bible class at Rhema Bible Church. Thank you for that opportunity—little did we know that leading hundreds of singles between the ages of 18-25 each week, would be the perfect preparation for pioneering and pastoring a church one day.

Troy and Joyce Wormell, Julie Werner and the Harrison House Publishers team; you brought me to the dance in 1994 and were the first to believe I had written something others needed to read when Harrison House published my first book, *Getting a Grip on the Basics*. A few decades later, look what the Lord has done! It's a joy to be working with all of you again. Thank you for believing in me and for sharing your expertise in publishing books that change the world. Eternity will tell a great story!

Finally, I am thankful for the godly men in my life—those I know well and those who are just acquaintances. First, thank you Jeff Jones for the millions of encouraging words! Thank you Dave Williams, Gerald Brooks, Tony Cooke, Sam Chand, John Hull, James O. Davis, Patrick Norris, Daniel Ho, Bruce Barton, Doug Jones and Ed Young—you didn't know it, but along the way, you've said something to me directly or in passing and

God used your words to encourage me more than you will ever know. Finally, thank you for support in endorsing this project Steve Kelly, Dennis Rouse and Keith Hudson. I also want to give a special thank you to my son-in-law Brodie Hock and my late father-in-law, Bill Jones for your kind words.

INTRODUCTION

It is my pleasure to introduce you to *Breaking Through the Stained Glass Ceiling.*

Are you ready, once and for all, to settle the question of the role of women in the church?

Can they teach, can they preach and can they lead? Why are we even asking these kinds of questions in the twenty-first century? As you open these pages, it's important to know that the words come from the pure heart of one who has served the Lord faithfully, forsaking building her own kingdom, but rather investing her life in His Church and the Kingdom to come.

I've had the extreme pleasure to witness those extraordinary gifts working through Beth Jones for nearly thirty years. As her husband and partner in ministry, I can attest to the fact that she is called by God and is a gifted communicator, strategist, and a proven executive. Her passion for God and His Church comes through all of her work. There is no one I know who works harder, cares more, or is more committed to fulfilling God's purpose for this life, and for making an eternal difference.

I read Galatians 3:28 and decided a long time ago that God wanted men and women to run together to build His Church in whatever roles He had called and gifted them to fulfill. "There is neither Jew nor Greek, there is neither slave nor free, there is neither male nor female; for you are all one in Christ Jesus..."

(NKJV). This book helps to bring to light the whole counsel of God's Word as it paints a wonderful picture of His plans to empower women for leadership within His Church.

I hope you'll join me in celebrating the gifts that God has given both men and women to work side by side to build Him a glorious Church without spot or wrinkle.

I pray—especially for you women—I hope you enjoy and are encouraged in the journey as you travel through these pages. For the men—husbands, dads, brothers—I pray you take time to read this book and receive fresh insight, greater respect and a new desire to encourage God's chosen women—your wife and the women, daughters or sisters in your own world.

Jeff Jones
Senior Pastor, Valley Family Church
Kalamazoo, Michigan

FOREWORD

I am excited that Beth has included me and my family in this wonderful project. The role of women in the church has always been an interesting topic, and it's an important one for the future health of the Church.

As a woman who has been involved in ministry for most of my life, I love to encourage people to run after their destiny. So, when Beth asked me to read the manuscript for *Breaking Through the Stained Glass Ceiling*, and included me as one of the profile stories in the book, I was honored and delighted to write the Foreword. As a teenager, I felt the call of God to teach the Bible and as a young woman, my father, the late Pastor John Osteen, greatly encouraged me to preach and fulfill my calling. He recognized the importance of women in ministry and was actually one of the first—if not the first—to involve my mother, Dodie Osteen, in the Lakewood Church services—speaking and praying for people. Since then, Pastors have followed suit in including their wives in ministry all over the world and enjoy working together to fulfill their calling.

Like many women who are involved in full time ministry, I have sometimes felt the need to justify my calling to others that may not agree with women having leadership roles in the Church. At the same time I have chosen to believe I am God's Masterpiece—created for a purpose and a destiny—and I have watched God bring my dreams to pass in His perfect timing! Even when I have not felt qualified, I have realized that God has chosen me and I am anointed, appointed, and approved by Him—and so are you. If you've had those same types of experiences, thoughts and dreams, you will be encouraged, inspired and empowered through reading this book.

In addition to the personal stories Beth, and other women leaders share in this book, her candid, Biblical approach to the questions that nobody wants to talk about will be a tremendous blessing to anyone struggling with the role of women in the church. She tackles each question with grace and does an excellent job backing each answer up with the Scripture.

I highly recommend this book to you. Beth is an excellent teacher, a leader and a gift to the Body of Christ and her insight allows others to see the importance of women in ministry today.

As you read these pages, I hope you hear the sound of shattered glass and remember—you are made for more!

Breaking through together,

Lisa Osteen Comes

Author, *You Are Made for More!*

Associate Pastor, Lakewood Church

2014

Chapter 1

THE ROLE OF WOMEN IN THE CHURCH

"I just want you to know; we're leaving the church."
She said it as such a matter of fact. I was stunned
and said, "Really? Why?"

At the time in 1992, my husband Jeff and I had been pioneering Kalamazoo Valley Family Church (now Valley Family Church) for about ten months when this young lady who had been faithfully serving as a lead teacher in our children's ministry, told me she and her husband were leaving the church.

"It's because of you," she said.

"Me? What did I do?" I asked, as I prepared to hear what I had done to force them out.

"My husband doesn't believe in women preachers," and with that, she turned and walked away.

I was surprised and hurt. It was a sock in the stomach. Her remarks that day were the first of many such opinions I would hear over the years. Little did I know how controversial this topic could be!

THE BIBLE SAYS WOMEN CAN'T...

I was raised as a Roman Catholic; our church leaders were priests and nuns—and the option of being a nun was never on my radar. When I became a born-again Christian, it was dramatic. Jesus radically changed my life! I loved Him. I loved following Him. I loved telling people about Him. When I felt God's call to the ministry, I didn't know what that would mean since I didn't have much experience with the evangelical world or the "controversy" over women preachers or leaders.

I was in for a rude awakening.

I quickly learned some familiar phrases that I'd come to dread: *"I don't believe in women preachers; so, how can you teach the Bible?" "Why does your husband let you teach the congregation? Doesn't the Bible say that women should be quiet in the church?" "You can teach the Bible, but only to other women—not to men—because you are supposed to be submissive and not have any authority over men." "My friends won't come to our church because we let women have leadership roles." "This conference is for the pastors (men)—the wives are going shopping."*

A few comments stand out. Years ago, one man was trying to give me a compliment—I think. After I had spoken on a Sunday morning, he walked right up to me and said, *"Personally, I don't care for women preachers, but my wife watches you on TV and she loves you."* I was almost encouraged!

I remember a comment card I received about a month after we moved into one of our new church buildings. It was in the middle of our Grand Opening celebration and the card had these encouraging words, *Why does she speak? She doesn't have anything to say!*

Many years ago, I received this email from a very genuine-hearted young man in our church:

> *I have been attending the church for a little while now. It is an amazing place to worship and I love it. But I recently invited my friend from work to come to the church with me. I told him the name and he said, 'Oh.' Then I asked him what was wrong with VFC. He replied with, 'They have a woman pastor.' I then questioned him. He told me to check out 1 Timothy 2:9-15, which talked about a woman's conduct inside the church. Wow. I do not understand, if it says that women should not speak in the church, then why do they? I am not at all jumping on you, because I love how you are bringing lots of people to Christ. But I do not understand and I was kind of hoping you could explain it to me and help me to understand . . . I'm probably not the first one to ask you about this, but if you could take the time out of your busy schedule to answer this for me, I'd very much appreciate it. I still want to attend the church because of the beautiful and wonderful things that are going on there, but I don't want to disobey God at all, in any way. If I can prevent myself from disobeying Him, I will. Thank you very much.*

I've learned that when people question or make disparaging statements about women in ministry, these comments are generally not intended to be personally hurtful—even though they hurt deeply. They are often the result of personal convictions or religious upbringing and traditions learned by sincere people who love God and His Word.

By the way, that couple? They did leave the church and I embarked on an interesting journey with the Lord and His call on my life.

THE STRUGGLE

Like thousands of women over the past several centuries, I've had many talks and tears with the Lord about this very topic, because in my heart I just wanted to please Him. I didn't want to disobey Him or His Word by thinking He had called me to lead and teach, when in reality He had not; nor did I want to disobey Him by not leading or teaching, when He had actually called me to do so.

To make matters more complicated, I felt strongly that the Lord wanted me to focus on leading and teaching *in* the church and writing books *for* the church. I've often felt conflicted about this and have asked God many times, *"Why have You called me to lead and teach in the church—the very place that doesn't believe in women like me?"* I've even tried on numerous occasions to get the Lord to release me from being focused on the church.

Eventually, like other women before me, I embraced what

I did not understand. Although it has not always made sense, God put a deep love and burden for the church—His Church—in my heart. I am convinced that serving the church is my sweet spot. It's my lane to run in. I'm a pioneer, a shepherd and a Bible teacher at heart. (After all, my maiden name was Beth Shepard, and as a young girl, I sometimes wondered if it described my destiny! Beth means "house of God" and Shepard is a variation on "shepherd"—so, there ya go!)

The truth is, I love the church, the global Church and local churches. I love seeing what the Holy Spirit does in people's lives through His Body, the church. I love everything the church is about: worship, evangelism, teaching, discipleship, relationships, transformation, growth, outreach, influence, creativity, healing, redemption and restoration, community, team, equipping and training! I love the way God uses His Church to bring the gospel to entire cities and regions.

I'm one of those people whose adrenaline gets pumping when we talk about church planting and church growth. Any time I see an empty building in any town around the world, my first instinct is to say, *"That would be a great place for a church"* and in an instant I envision a church taking up residence there. Whenever I have a creative idea for reaching people with the gospel, it is always connected to the church. When I write a book, my driving motivation is always, "How will this help the church help people?"

I get happy and fired up every time I read this passage about the power of His Church:

"All this energy issues from Christ: God raised him from death and set him on a throne in deep heaven, in charge of running the universe, everything from galaxies to governments, no name and no power exempt from his rule. And not just for the time being, but forever. He is in charge of it all, has the final word on everything. **At the center of all this, Christ rules the church. The church, you see, is not peripheral to the world; the world is peripheral to the church.** *The church is Christ's body, in which he speaks and acts, by which he fills everything with his presence." (Ephesians 1:20-23, MSG, emphasis mine)*

Over the past 30-plus years, I've studied the Scriptures and the various theological arguments on the subject of women in ministry, and teaching and leading in the church. I've spoken to other godly people about this subject. I've read books by Christian men I highly respected and I've listened to sermon messages on this topic. I've prayed. I've lived it. I've learned a few things. This book is about what I've come to understand from the Word and my own personal experience about the sometimes controversial role of women in the church.

Questions, misunderstandings and comments have led to confusion and hurt for many women who have sensed God's hand on their lives and a strong call to serve Him with the leadership, executive, strategic, visionary and teaching gifts He's given them. Some have given up and any dreams they've had have wilted and died a painful, quiet death under the stained glass. Others live in a perpetual state of disappointment knowing how much they could bring to the table in helping their husbands and their churches, if only they were given freedom to use their leadership gifts. Still others have revolted in their own version of "pastors' wives gone wild" and have kissed the church goodbye.

I trust the lessons learned by me and the other women leaders profiled in this book will help those of you who feel called of God to teach, preach and lead in the church, but are restrained by the stained glass ceiling. I am also hopeful these pages will shed some light on this subject for the men who read this book.

WHY THIS BOOK NOW?

It's time. Time for thousands of women (and perhaps men) to settle these questions: What roles should women have in the church? Does the overarching counsel of God's Word teach that women must be silent in the church? Does the Bible teach that women cannot teach or preach in the church? Is it true that women are not supposed to teach men? Is it true that women are not to have any spiritual leadership role in the church?

This is a book about: Women. Leadership. Church. But, it's not a book just for women. It's a book for anyone interested in what could happen if thousands of women—called and gifted—were welcomed into leadership along with men in local churches around the globe to reach people for Christ and turn our church monuments in movements that will have a greater impact on this world.

This is a fresh biblical view of a topic that has been hotly contested for millennia. For those who are wondering what could help the church regain its relevance and influence in cities around the globe—this may be a huge missing piece and a secret weapon God wants to release in this hour.

This book is my story and the stories of a dozen other high capacity women called to leadership in churches around the world—and it's giving a voice to thousands of other women who have prayed, worked, cried and carried on as they seek to serve the Lord and fulfill His calling on their lives.

I will be the first to admit that this book is not an exhaustive theological treatise on this subject. I do not address every verse of Scripture that relates to the role of women in ministry and church life and I may raise more questions than I answer. I also understand the fact that because I, as a woman, am writing this book, it could be perceived as biased from the start. I get that. As a "male counter-balance," I have listed many excellent resources created by men on the subject of a woman's role in the church at the end of the book, and I highly recommend them.

In the same way that a male gynecologist who's delivered many babies can give authoritative, expert advice on having a baby, a woman who's delivered six children has a different take on what it's like to have a baby. They both speak with the authority of their perspective. He speaks with a medical authority, and she speaks with a different kind of authority. This book may fit into that category—a different look at this important Biblical subject. So, I hope you'll join me to the very last page as we explore the role of women in the church.

HOW I GOT HERE

Let me start by sharing a bit of my story. I hope that through sharing my experience—we can get acquainted and those of you who are on a similar journey will be encouraged in knowing you are not alone.

It was 1979. I was minding my own business when God tapped me. The idea of being in the ministry or involved in a church at any level was not a thought I had *ever* considered as a teen or young adult. My life goals were simple: attend college, major in biology, become a dentist, get married, have five kids (who would all wear matching outfits on Easter) and play tennis.

As a freshman in college, I figured I would just have a good time, get my degree, go to dental school and live the life I envisioned. But God had a different idea. First, He used Andrea, my childhood friend and college roommate to lead me to Christ. When Jesus came into my life, everything changed—especially my life goals and priorities. My number one goal, as the oldest of four sisters being raised by a single mom, was to lead the rest of my family to the Lord. Within a short few years, this was accomplished and everyone in my family had given their lives to Jesus, yet the idea of leadership in the church was still non-existent.

The only experience I had being a "leader" in church after I was born again started and ended after one of the most embarrassing moments of my life. It was Sunday. My mom and stepdad were already at church and I was supposed to meet them, but running late. I wanted my new dress to look perfect, so it took me a little longer than usual to get ready, but I finally made it to church when the worship leader was starting the second song. Everyone was standing as I looked around the sanctuary to spot my parents—yep, there they were in the second row. I made my way to the pew and stood there along with everyone else praising the Lord and feeling pretty good about this new dress and myself.

When our pastor told us to "turn and greet and have a seat," I made sure I greeted everyone to the north, south, east and west of me—after all, they needed to see how good I was looking! When I went to sit down, I smoothed my dress under my behind, only to discover something was missing—primarily, my dress! Unknowingly, in my hurry, I had tucked my dress and my slip into my panty hose. I sat down and tried to figure out a way to untuck. Then I began to go through the list, *Who's behind me? Who saw me walk down the aisle? How long was I standing there with my hands in the air and my 'tush' exposed?* I was mortified and humiliated! I have no idea what our pastor preached on that day. That experience sealed it—the idea of being a "leader" in church was not something I desired...at all!

That changed one afternoon in 1979. I was a sophomore in college at Western Michigan University and while sitting in my dorm room and meeting with Debbie, the Campus Crusade for Christ Group Leader who was mentoring me, God interrupted my plans! She shared a little book with me titled: *Have You Discovered God's Plan for Your Life?* I had not discovered God's plan. I didn't even know God had a plan. I figured God would bless my plan, and my plan was to become a dentist! As she was reading that booklet to me, she came to Romans 10:13-15 and it jumped off the page;

*"'Everyone who calls on the name of the Lord will
be saved.' How, then, can they call on the one they
have not believed in? And how can they believe in
the one of whom they have not heard? And how
can they hear without someone preaching to them?
And how can anyone preach unless they are sent?
As it is written: 'How beautiful are the feet of those
who bring good news!'" (NIV).*

Time stood still for a few moments and I suddenly knew
God was calling me. This was a monumental moment. I knew
I couldn't be a dentist. If God was just looking for preachers—
people who would tell others how to not spend an eternity apart
from Him—how could I be a dentist and let people go to hell?

The way I saw it, if all people needed to do in order to be
saved was to call on the name of the Lord, and if the only reason
they hadn't called on the name of the Lord was because they had
not heard, then, I had to tell them. It seemed as if God spoke
to my heart with a huge announcement: *"I interrupt your life to
bring you this very important message. You are not going to be a
dentist. You are going to tell people about Me."* From that moment
on, my life and purpose changed!

Although I had no idea what being called to the ministry
would actually look like, somehow I knew that the primary way
I would be telling people about Jesus would be through writing
and teaching, and that one day when I got married, I would be
working together with my husband to build a church and raise
a family.

MY STORY IS PROBABLY A LOT LIKE YOUR STORY

As it turned out, this has indeed been God's plan for my life. I left Western Michigan University, transferred to Boston University and changed my major to learn all I could about Communications and Public Relations—for the purpose of preaching the gospel. After I graduated from college, I spent several years serving the Lord through various campus ministries, churches and non-profit organizations. Then I received my ministry training from Rhema Bible Training College.

In the process of time, I met my husband Jeff and after we were married, we did start a family—and a church—and I've been teaching and writing books. We had four children—well, actually five if you count the church!

When it comes to our family—Jeff and I love the privilege of being parents and I can say without hesitation, our kids have been our most important ministry and our greatest joy! Meghan, our oldest daughter, was three years old, Annie was ten months old, and I was pregnant with our third child, Luke, when we pioneered Valley Family Church in 1991 in Kalamazoo, Michigan. Three years later in 1994, we had our youngest son, Eric. Pioneering a church while raising four preschoolers meant that I was pregnant for about six years in a row, and Jeff and I lived with one nostril above water. Sleep was worth more than money. We leaned on God's "grace for the pace" daily and loved every second of it! (Well, maybe not *every* second.)

We were a little nervous about raising "pastor's kids!" Neither Jeff nor I were raised in a pastor's home, so we were clueless how to do this. You've probably heard stories about pastor's families and "pks," pastor's kids. We did too! Horror stories! That's what freaked us out! Since we didn't know what the "proper protocol" was, we just did our best to work at having a fun family, enjoying our marriage and raising kids who loved God and others. We had two major rules in our home: *You can't call anyone 'stupid' and whatever you do, first ask, 'Would this please the Lord?'* We weren't perfect and our kids weren't perfect but our approach seemed to work, and now that our kids are young adults, the verdict is in—our kids turned out to be really nice people. They love God and they all feel called to the ministry and are actively serving as leaders in our church. We have no complaints! Our family is one of the most rewarding things God has blessed us with. Then, there is that fifth child...

It turns out that Valley Family Church was our fifth child—we didn't realize it at the time—but in truth, she was! She was a growing child—demanding and strong-willed—we loved her with all our heart and she brought great joy into our lives! We gave birth to VFC with five adults and four kids and since that time, our church has grown to include thousands of people who call us home—along with a couple of campus launches and a church plant.

From the beginning, we felt it was our job to build a multi-generational church that would help people "get it". In simple terms, our church exists: *to help people get it,* and that means...

> *The lost get saved.*
> *The saved get victory.*
> *The victorious get trained.*
> *The trained get going.*

Our goal was to build a church that would successfully blend reaching lost, unchurched people; while at the same time, equipping believers to live the Spirit-filled life of faith so they could reach out to more lost and unchurched people. This is no easy task. For some, our church isn't deep enough, for others we are too deep. Perhaps this is a compliment?

The best and only way we know to measure our effectiveness is: fruit! Forty-percent of those who attend our church tell us they were not attending church anywhere prior to coming to our church—that makes us very happy! Those who did know the Lord before attending our church tell us they are growing at an exponential rate as God's Word comes alive in their hearts. The fruit we've seen in people coming to know Jesus Christ and the spiritual growth we've seen in their lives of others has truly been *"our joy and our crown!"*

In order to raise our own four children (Meghan, Annie, Luke, Eric) and our fifth child—Valley Family Church, we felt God called us to work together as a husband-wife team. In our roles at home, we are "mom and dad" and we share all that goes with raising a busy family. In our roles as the senior pastors, we are the "spiritual mom and dad" of the House and we share all that goes with raising a busy church family. We have our unique gifts, responsibilities and roles and yet, we work on many things together, including: teaching, strategy and execution. We cast vision, lead the staff and oversee the church as a husband and wife team and since 2003, we have split the weekend preaching 50/50. God has blessed our approach in leading our family and church as we have endeavored to live by Psalm 34:3, *"Oh, magnify the LORD with me, and let us exalt his name together."*

Thankfully, we've had help! The Lord has surrounded us with a great staff and team of volunteers. Early on, He called several special people to help us at home with our kids—and we are forever indebted to them. The Lord has called hundreds of other people to use their gifts to come alongside and help us build a church. Like most pastors, we feel that we have the best staff, lay leaders, volunteers and church family in the world! As a church, we have lived on God's fulfillment to His promise to command His blessing on our church as we all walk in unity, *"Behold, how good and how pleasant it is for brethren to dwell together in unity... For there the LORD commanded the blessing— life forevermore" (Psalm 133:1, 3).*

In addition to my role in working together with my husband to pioneer and grow the church, as I mentioned, a large part of my calling has been to write books to help people get the basics. God has enabled me to write around twenty books, including, the *7 Basics* and the *Getting a Grip* on the Basics series, which are being used by hundreds of churches in America and have been translated into over a dozen foreign languages around the world.

So, that's part of my story. I'll share more later.

GUTTER BALLS

As you can see, although serving God in ministry was not on my original radar, I eventually figured out how to accept, embrace and step into God's calling to be a leader in our church. But to be honest, it was a process—and I had to learn how to quit throwing "gutter balls."

In the early years of planting our church, I was idealistic, optimistic and certain that everyone would want to help us win all of Southwest Michigan to Jesus. But after a few years of pioneering, I got weary of being rejected by those who did not approve of my role. Their negative comments wore me down to the point that for a few years, I let insecurity, intimidation, and the "fear of man" dominate me and I threw "gutter balls." That is, I backed off from following my heart, passion and purpose. I shrank back from doing much of anything public that looked like leadership, being on the platform or teaching God's Word. I threw gutter balls so I would not appear to be a leader.

Let me explain a gutter ball. When I was in junior high school, a group of us boys and girls went bowling one day. My mother taught my sisters and me a simple rule of thumb: *". . . in sports, don't beat the boys."* (It was a different era then. I don't know too many teenage girls that would embrace that philosophy these days!)

Normally I wasn't a very good bowler, but that day I must have been in the zone because I found myself bowling strikes and spares. However, I knew if I continued to bowl well, I'd beat the boys and that was a "no-no." So, what did I do? I started throwing gutter balls—on purpose! I marched up to the line, acted like I was trying to get a strike, and then at the last minute I'd throw my bowling ball toward one of the gutters to make sure I didn't win.

Sadly, that mentality resurfaced as I navigated my role as a woman in church leadership. I had "reluctant leader syndrome." At times, it was just easier to throw a "ministry gutter ball" and not step up to the plate, or God's calling, in order to avoid being criticized. Fortunately, my husband wouldn't let me throw gutter balls for too long. He has always been my biggest encourager, and his consistent support has been immeasurable.

In addition to my husband's words of wisdom, my greatest comfort has been in sensing God's encouragement and approval. One day, as I drove around Kalamazoo praying for our city, I was feeling particularly "gutter-ball-minded" and the Lord quickened this verse to me, *"Do not be afraid, but speak, and do not keep silent; for I am with you, and no one will attack you to hurt you; for I have many people in this city" (Acts 18:9-10, NKJV).*

As I embraced this word, my heart was anchored. God has confirmed His calling time and time again. Every now and then I'll hear Him speaking, almost singing this Glen Miller song to my heart, *"I've got a gal in Kalamazoo..."* Knowing that I am "His gal" makes all the difference, and is a great source of encouragement in my calling.

STAINED GLASS OR A CONCRETE AND REBAR CEILING?

You've heard my story, but what about yours?

I know you are out there because I have talked to hundreds of you. It's possible that in your organization or church world, the "stained glass ceiling" isn't made of stained glass, but of concrete and rebar. The idea of leading or teaching the Word to others is in a galaxy far, far away. Maybe you don't feel called to pastoral ministry, teaching or preaching, but you do feel that your leadership gifts and passion for the cause of Christ could serve the church in other ways—through creative arts, worship, media, communications, executive operations, connections, spiritual development, finance, kids and student ministries, outreach, technological, legal or justice initiatives or a host of other areas—if only you were given the chance.

In a galaxy far, far away...

I understand. We've seen it . . . and you've seen it. Women— who are tremendous wives and mothers, as well as spiritually mature and anointed with wisdom, faith, leadership, executive, administrative, organizational, creative, entrepreneurial and/or teaching gifts, and have paid their "faithfulness" dues—seem to be stuck in an orbit which only includes creating the bulletin, singing in the choir, playing the piano, hosting showers, doing secretarial work or making chicken divan casseroles for funerals,

An added dilemma for high-potential, high-capacity women

called to the ministry is to watch ill-equipped, immature, incompetent, and inexperienced men move up the leadership ladder in church, passing by exceptionally qualified, godly women—simply or only because they are men.

The result of this standard operating procedure in the church is that many gifted, called, and anointed women have given up and are using their gifts outside the church. They've been accepted as lawyers, brain surgeons, dentists, accountants, editors, broadcast journalists, engineers, architects, entertainers, film-makers, designers, entrepreneurs, university presidents, CEOs, governors, senators, prime ministers and presidents; but they have been banned from leadership in many churches. What a loss for the global Body of Christ and local churches everywhere.

Is that really God's plan?

HANG IN THERE

Girls, what about you? Is the cause of Christ what you are most passionate about? Is God's Word burning in your heart like a fire shut up in your bones? Has God wired you to be a pioneer, innovator, church planter, campus pastor, teacher, preacher or leader in the church?

Are you discouraged because no one has validated your call as authentic and God-given? Do you feel pregnant with a vision and about to burst? Are you a woman who's felt God's call to the ministry—but you've experienced so much disapproval, rejection or criticism, you've given up? Have you been given limited opportunities to do what's in your heart, but it's usually the role no one else wants and there's no budget to support it? Have you prayed for God to just "take away" your desire to proclaim His Word? Have you asked the Lord if He gave you the wrong gifts? Have you faced the frustration of closed-door-after-closed-door in your local church? Have you felt despised, overlooked or misunderstood? Have you been tolerated, but not accepted? Have you been dismayed by the critics? Have you been throwing "gutter balls" or living in a state of perpetual "reluctant leader" syndrome? Perhaps you can relate to one or all of these questions. If you've had high hopes and extreme patience, I know that the deferral of your hope can make your heart sick. Hang in there! Don't give up! God hasn't forgotten about you.

Don't quit. Don't give up!

Let me encourage you. Shifts are happening in both the global and local church. I don't know how or when, but you can trust the Lord. He has your back. The Bible says, *"And I thank Christ Jesus our Lord who has enabled me, because He counted me faithful, putting me into the ministry"* (1 Timothy 1:12, NKJV). Don't be discouraged! If God is for you, who can be against you? Stay faithful! Do what you know to do. He will produce eternal fruit through your life and eventually others will recognize His hand upon you. The most important thing isn't the approval of man, but the approval that comes from God.

It's my prayer as we tackle this topic, *breaking through the stained glass ceiling*, that you sense the Lord encouraging you, strengthening you, and filling you with renewed hope in your calling.

> *The LORD will guide you continually, and satisfy
> your soul in drought, and strengthen your bones;
> you shall be like a watered garden, and like a spring
> of water, whose waters do not fail* (Isaiah 58:11,
> NKJV).

Let's take a look at the Word, women, and the church in this modern culture.

CHAPTER 2

THIS ONE'S FOR THE GIRLS

If you want to start a fight in church, initiate a conversation about women preachers and within 45 minutes, you can split that church four ways! As every woman in a high profile role in the church knows, there are many different views on this subject. Those views often carry strong emotions.

Years ago, I led a man to the Lord and as I spoke with him on numerous occasions, he told me in no uncertain terms that he didn't believe in women preachers, further, he was not interested in attending our church, reading any of the books I had written or hearing me teach or preach the Word. One day, he went so far as to tell me I was not even saved. As it turns out, this man was my dad. Of course, his words cut deeply and I had to seek God's help to tune them out and look to my Heavenly Father and His Words to carry on in His calling. (Today, my dad is in heaven and I have the hope that he sees things differently now.)

My guess is that if you are a woman in leadership or in a teaching or preaching role in the church, you've had similar experiences. And, if you're like me, while there are a few naysayers, God finds a way to trump them all with His still small voice and by prompting people to speak kind and encouraging words just when you need it. (In fact, I hope you hear the Lord's still small voice and sense His love and affirmation for you personally as you read these pages!)

In writing this book, it is not my goal to defend, argue or convince anyone of anything. My primary goal in writing is to inspire, empower, encourage and cheer for you young girls and older women who have felt alone, rejected and misunderstood as you seek to follow God's call on your lives. My goal for all other readers is that they simply consider looking at this topic with a fresh set of eyes.

This book is written for...

Women of All Ages: It's written to encourage and motivate women of all ages who feel called of God to change the world—to break through the stained glass ceiling—to pioneer churches, teach the Word, write books, start ministries, lead worship or serve as leaders in churches.

Men of All Distinctions: It's written to enlighten men who have a wife with an insatiable hunger for serving God and teaching the Word. It's written to help the father whose daughter has a heart for the Lord and potential leadership or speaking gifts. It's written for brothers with sisters and boyfriends with girlfriends who feel called to the ministry.

Church Leaders of All Breeds: It's written to encourage pastors or church leaders who are unsure of, or are rethinking, the role of women in their own churches.

Many people are giving this topic considerable thought these days and thankfully, more and more Christian leaders see the value of women in the church. In this chapter, let's lay some groundwork and then we'll dive into the Scriptures.

BIG MINISTRIES

As we begin, it's worth mentioning that some of the largest, most influential and effective ministries and churches around the world have placed a high value on women and their role in the church.

Despite some recent setbacks, the largest church in the world, Yoido Full Gospel Central, located in Seoul, Korea with a 2014 membership of 1,000,000 members,[1] has been built largely by women in leadership through cell groups according to Pastor David Yonggi Cho (formerly known as Paul Yonggi Cho).

He began to see that by doing everything himself he was robbing his people of the chance to grow. From this he learned the importance of delegation and of training up the people for the work of the ministry. Cho then went on to devise his plan to minister to the people through a network of home cells and using the people to lead them. He took this plan to the deacons, but they said no. He then took the idea to the deaconesses and they accepted it. They realized that the biggest problem with this was going to be for the men to come under the authority of women leaders. Women in Korea had always taken a subordinate role and as Cho says, 'There is no feminist movement in Korea.' They overcame this problem by having the women wear caps to signify that they were under Cho's authority. Using the women as leaders they started with 20 home cells. This quickly grew to 150 groups. [2]

Joyce Meyer, one of the most widely read, listened to, and well-known female Bible teachers in the world today, is being used by God to reach millions of people through TV, radio, and books.

Joyce Meyer is one of the world's leading practical Bible teachers and a New York Times bestselling author, spreading God's Word to millions of people each year. Suffering sexual abuse as a child, Joyce discovered the freedom to live victoriously by applying God's Word to her life and, in turn, seeks to help others do the same. She has written over 70 books, conducts close to fifteen conferences annually, and reaches a potential audience of 3 billion people worldwide with her Enjoying Everyday Life® broadcast. Time magazine selected Joyce as one of the most influential evangelical leaders in America. [3]

Australian Darlene Zschech's biography reads like a woman who is being mightily used of the Lord through serving in leadership, pastoral ministry and preaching via song.

Darlene Zschech is acclaimed all over the world as a singer, songwriter, worship leader and speaker, most notably for spearheading the music that comes from Hillsong Church. Although she has achieved numerous gold albums and her songs are sung in many nations of the world, her success simply stands as a testimony to her life's passion to serve God and people with all her heart. Darlene, alongside her husband Mark, are Senior Pastors of Hope Unlimited Church on the Central Coast of New South Wales, Australia.

As a songwriter, Darlene is perhaps most famous for the chorus "Shout to the Lord," a song that is sung by millions of churchgoers every week and has been covered by many other artists. "Shout to the Lord" was nominated as Album of the Year for the 1997 Dove Awards and was nominated as Song of the Year for the 1998 Dove Awards. In 2000, Darlene received a Dove Award nomination for Songwriter of the Year and received the International Award for influence in praise and worship.

Darlene is also passionate about raising and training other worship pastor, leaders, teams and writers and has written four books – "Extravagant Worship," "The Kiss of Heaven," "The Art of Mentoring" and the new "Revealing Jesus" devotional. These titles combined have been translated into over 20 different languages. [4]

Henrietta Mears, simply known as "Teacher" to countless men and women, was the Director of Christian Education and the teacher of the College Department at the First Presbyterian Church of Hollywood from 1928-1963. She also founded Gospel Light Publications and Gospel Literature International, which have been used around the world to bring gospel publications to thousands of churches. Such notables as Dr. Billy Graham, Senator Mark Hatfield, Dr. Charles Fuller, Dale Rogers, and the late Dawson Trotman (founder of The Navigators) and the late

Dr. Bill Bright (founder of Campus Crusade for Christ) were impacted by her influence as a Bible teacher, church leader and godly woman in an era where women had very few rights.[5]

Dr. Bill Bright had this to say about her influence in his life, *"I have had the privilege of knowing many godly pastors and great Christian leaders, but no one has influenced my life more than Dr. Mears."*[6] Dr. Richard Halverson, Chaplain to the United States Senate said this, *"In my mind, Henrietta Mears was the giant of Christian education-not only in her generation, but in this century. She was an extraordinary combination of intellect, devotion, and spirituality; an administrative genius, a motivator, an encourager and a leader. I thought of Henrietta Mears as a female Apostle Paul; in fact, I often referred to her as the 'Epistle Paul.' There is simply no way to exaggerate her effectiveness as a teacher, communicator and inspirer."*[7]

In modern times, I have had the distinct pleasure of meeting Jo Anne Lyon, the first woman to serve in the top leadership role of the Wesleyan denomination as the General Superintendent. She serves to guide the vision, key message, and missional priorities of the Wesleyan Church, which is transforming lives, churches, and communities with the hope and holiness of Jesus Christ.

She speaks with grace and wisdom and carries a strong, strategic, leadership anointing. She is passionate about what God is doing in calling women to the ministry in unprecedented numbers these days, both those in college and seminaries as well as second-career women.

In her recent article, "Men and Women - An Article on Spirit-Filled Believers" she said this,

> *In the tour of a church in Ft. Worth, Texas, that has set the pace for planting churches and reaching the world in the most difficult places my eyes fell on a painting hanging in the hallway. I was captured by what appeared to be the backs of a crowd of people shrouded in grey. However, there was one person in red. The pastor explained: this represents a woman who pastors a church of 100,000 – yes, I did not add a zero – in North Vietnam. The artist depicted her among the crowds of people who do not know Jesus as the one who is "covered by the blood."*

> *I stood before that painting with eyes filled with tears. The courage of this woman to proclaim the gospel in a place of persecution! The faith of this woman to know Jesus and the power of the resurrection! The obvious attraction and hope of Jesus through her!*

> *I then reflected on the thousands of women who are church planters in China, many between the ages of 18-24 with some 30 million followers. Again, the courage, faith and power of the Holy Spirit make this possible.*

> *I was again drawn to the words of Joel which were preached by Peter at Pentecost:*

> *"In the last days, God says, I will pour out my Spirit on all people. Your sons and daughters will prophesy, your young men will see visions, your old*

men will dream dreams. Even on my servants, both men and women, I will pour out my Spirit in those days, and they will prophesy" (Acts 2:17-18 NIV).

God is calling women to the ministry in unprecedented numbers these days, both those in college and seminaries as well as second-career women. Whether they are in North Vietnam and China, or Virginia and Canada, I believe a new Pentecost is rising with them.[8]

I also want to mention Bill Hybels, the founder and pastor of the influential Willow Creek Church. I have never had the pleasure of personally meeting Bill Hybels (although he is from Kalamazoo and graduated from the high school our children attended), but he has been a champion for women in ministry since the earliest days of Willow Creek's existence. On Twitter, he posted links to two very moving, must-read articles; one written by he and his wife, Lynne, and the other written by their daughter, Shauna. I must admit that I had a hard time reading these articles because of the lump in my throat and the tears in my eyes. They put into such eloquent words the things I and many other women have experienced in their callings to serve God in ministry and in leadership in the church. If you are a woman who feels called to the ministry and to leadership in the church, I implore you to read both of these articles. Here's an excerpt from Bill and Lynne Hybels' article, "Evangelicals and Gender Equality," regarding the time they had to define their position on women in church leadership.

...the increasing visibility of Willow in secular and Christian media forced us to define and articulate our position. Questions began pouring in about why we "allowed" women in leadership. Did we have a rational defense for our position? In response, we commissioned our elders to do an intensive, eighteen-month scriptural study of the issue of women in leadership. I did not feel it was right to sideline the women whom God seemed to be using while we did this study, so we pursued a parallel track of study and continued observation of how God worked among us through the leadership efforts of both men and women.

Dr. Gilbert Bilezikian, a Wheaton College professor and Willow Creek elder, led the study. The conclusions of the study were published in 1985 in Bilezikian's book, Beyond Sex Roles: What the Bible Says about a Woman's Place in Church and Family. In summary, we concluded that before the Fall, men and women related to each other as co-regents, both bearing the image of God and called to join together in caring for the world he had created. Both men and women were responsible to fulfill their ministries of service for God's glory in the manner God had gifted them and to the degree to which they had been apportioned faith. Tragically, in the Fall, this cooperative relationship between men and women was deeply wounded. We believe God's gracious plan for redemption is that everything that was broken through sin—including the relationship between men and women—might be restored to the beauty that existed during the first days of Creation.

Many devout, intelligent Christians disagree with our conclusions. There will come a day when we will all find out the degree to which we have veered from God's perfect wisdom, in this issue and many others. Until then, I hold this position humbly, yet firmly. I am willing to take the risk of encouraging women to do what I believe scriptures ask of them— to make themselves fully available to the full range of spiritual gifts. [9]

There is no doubt that God has richly blessed Pastor Cho, Joyce Meyer, Darlene Zschech, Henrietta Mears, Jo Anne Lyon, Bill and Lynne Hybels and their ministries—and a growing list of other ministries and churches where women have been given a high profile in leading, teaching and preaching.

LEAVING A LEGACY

Perhaps you can think of other legacy-leaving women preachers, teachers and leaders. Aimee Semple Mcpherson was a woman ahead of her time, as an evangelist and founder of the Foursquare Denomination in the early 1900's.[10] Maria B. Woodworth-Etter was an evangelist well-known in the Assemblies of God circles for her dynamic preaching and life of faith.[11] Kathryn Kuhlman was greatly used of God. She was known for her dramatic preaching and healing ministry which began in the late 1940's and later for her radio and television ministry. When asked, "What do you regard as the ultimate goal of your ministry?" She replied: "My purpose is the salvation of souls. Divine healing is secondary to the transformation of a life."[12]

In modern times, Bishop T.D. Jakes has been championing the role of women through his conferences and bestselling book, *"Woman Thou Art Loosed."*[13] Pastor Bobbie Houston, married to Pastor Brian Houston from Hillsong Church in Australia, has been leading and empowering an army of tens of thousands of women through her annual Colour Conferences.[14]

Nancy Beach is a pioneer among women leaders in the church and serves as the executive vice president of programming and production for the Willow Creek Association, a teaching pastor at Willow Creek Community Church and is the author of *Gifted to Lead: The Art of Leading as a Woman in the Church*. Nancy has been blazing a trail for many years. She is still hopeful regarding the role of women in the church and she had this to say about her role as a woman in leadership in her honest article titled, "Women in Leadership—Disappointed, but Not Despairing."[15]

> *Almost 30 years ago when I started serving on staff as a church leader, my role on the Management Team was somewhat pioneering, at least for our church. As the first female on that team, and later, the first female Teaching Pastor, I sought to do the work of ministry as best I could, hoping that my gender would actually not be a big deal or a barrier. I am deeply grateful for the opportunities I had, for the adventure of learning in the trenches of leadership, for the men and women who opened up a place for me at the table and made room for my voice...*

For decades, God has used noted Christian leaders and Bible teachers like these powerhouses: Kay Arthur, Gloria Copeland,

Anne Graham Lotz, Marilyn Hickey, Lynette Hagin, Jill Briscoe, Anne Gimenez, Sheila Walsh, Stormie Omartian, and Jeanne Mayo and in their respective spheres of influence to teach the Word of God to thousands of women (and men) in churches, Bible Schools and auditoriums around the world.

These days, there are many more women taking their place in the global church. Women leaders like, Lisa Bevere, speaker and author of *Girls with Swords;* Pricilla Shirer, author of *God is Able,* Beth Moore, author of *Breaking Free;* Victoria Osteen, author of *Love Your Life; and* Lisa Osteen Comes, author of *You Are Made for More* are raising the bar for women.

Then, there's Christine Caine and Nancy Alcorn—women on the front lines! Chris Caine is a preacher, advocate and author of *Undaunted*, who champions the church everywhere she goes and who also founded the A21 Campaign, an anti-human trafficking organization that fights slavery around the globe. Nancy Alcorn has been blazing a trail as a leader in the church since 1983 when she founded Mercy Ministries, dedicated to serving young women between the ages of 13-28. Nancy and her team help young women who face a combination of life-controlling issues such as eating disorders, self-harm, drug and alcohol addictions, depression and unplanned pregnancy. Mercy also serves young women who have been physically and sexually abused, including victims of sex trafficking. Using proven methods, a holistic approach and professional counselors in a structured residential environment, Mercy has helped thousands of young women be restored to wholeness.[16]

And...the list goes on. (I hesitate to name names because there are so many women who deserve to be recognized and mentioned and I don't want anyone to feel overlooked. God knows who you are!) Just add the names of thousands upon thousands of other incredible, off-the-charts women who serve as church leaders, pastors, pastors wives, Bible teachers, pioneers, missionaries, prayer warriors, authors, worship leaders, innovators and influencers to the list—and it's easy to see that God is up to something!

The point is—it's exciting and refreshing to see God's hand of favor and blessing on a variety of established and up-and-coming Christian women leaders who are being used globally, nationally, regionally and in their local churches.

And, you are one of them!

THIS IS YOUR TIME!

I hope you are being encouraged by these stories, ladies! The Lord is on your side. If God is for you, who can be against you? As you live to please the Lord and walk in humility and obedience to Him, He will fulfill His will in your lives.

I especially want to cheer for you young women—those in your teens, 20s, and 30s. If you sense God's hand on your life for the ministry of preaching the gospel, pioneering Christian endeavors, leadership in the church and/or teaching the Word, be encouraged. You are living in some of the best days ever for being a woman in ministry! Stay strong in your relationship with the Lord and walk in humility and wisdom. Seek counsel from godly men and women in your life, so you can experience all God has called you to be and do in Him!

I also want to encourage you ladies in your 40s, 50s, 60s, 70s (and even 80s) as you think about the second-half of your life. Maybe you're approaching retirement from your career, or perhaps your kids are grown and you're wondering what your empty nest years are supposed to look like. It's not too late for you! At this season of your life, you have history with God, wisdom, and life experience that will greatly help others. The younger generation needs you to be out front leading and serving as "spiritual mothers" who will encourage, nurture, teach, train and model godly Christianity, leadership in prayer and being sold-out to God.

HISTORICAL CROSSROADS

Did you know that this is the first time in history when five of the largest generations ever are alive and in their prime? Just think about the strategic power in that. What could God do if the women from young Generation Z (born after 2001), the energetic Millennials (born between 1981-2001), the smart GenXers (born between 1965-1980), the experienced Baby Boomers (born between 1946-1964) and the wise women from the Greatest Generation (born between 1922-1945) were released to join forces with one another—and the men in their lives—to proclaim the gospel and build churches? Don't shrink back girls. The church needs you! The world needs you!

Ladies, this is your time. You don't have to throw gutter balls any longer. On the other hand, you don't need to become a masculine "she-man" to do what God has called you to do. It's not your job to promote yourself, be domineering, or "wear the pants." You don't need to defend yourself, whine or pout. You don't have to be overbearing, hyper-spiritual, controlling or manipulative in your desire to serve the Lord in ministry. Just continue to seek after God, walk in love, live by His Word, stay full of the spirit, remain humble and be bold in doing what He's called you to do—the fruit of your life and ministry will speak for itself.

It's a new era and there are more opportunities across denominational lines for women to serve the Lord with their God-given gifts and callings.

It's time!

It was prophesied of you many, many years ago. *"In the last days, God says, I will pour out my Spirit on all people.* **Your sons and daughters will prophesy**, *your young men will see visions, your old men will dream dreams.* **Even on my servants, both men and women,** *I will pour out my Spirit in those days, and* **they will prophesy**" (Acts 2:17-18, NIV, emphasis mine).

GOD'S WORD IS THE BOTTOM LINE

As women who sense God's call on our lives to lead, teach, or preach, we are ultimately accountable to God and His Word—not our personal experiences or the opinions of others. So, what does God say in His Word about this subject? Does the Bible command women to be silent and unable to lead in the church?

Rightly divide the Word.

We are exhorted to "rightly" divide the Word of truth, *"Be diligent to present yourself approved to God, a worker who does not need to be ashamed, **rightly dividing the word of truth**" (2 Timothy 2:15, NKJV, emphasis mine).* If we are not diligent in our study of the Word, we may inadvertently "wrongly" divide the Word and make it say something it did not intend to say. It's a great comfort to know that as we study God's Word, the Holy Spirit will reveal His wisdom to us.

In our next chapter, we will compare Scripture with Scripture to discover what God has said about women teaching, preaching, and leading in His Church.

Before we move on to Chapter 3, let's take a look at an inspiring group of women leaders who are serving God in the church: *The Osteen Girls.*

WOMEN LEADERS IN THE CHURCH: THE OSTEEN GIRLS

April Osteen Simons, Tamara Osteen Graff,
Dodie Osteen and Lisa Osteen Comes

Victoria Osteen

Jennifer Osteen

I have had the distinct pleasure of meeting most of the Osteen girls over the years—if only for a few moments—and have had the chance to spend some extended time with Tamera Osteen Graff working together on a few projects. I am especially honored that Lisa Osteen Comes, a woman who has spent so much of her life leading, teaching and serving the Lord in and through the local church was willing to write such a nice foreword for this book. Anyone who has ever met or spent any time with the Osteens would agree that it doesn't take more than a minute to see they are the real deal and some of the kindest people and most compassionate families alive. They aren't a perfect family—they are the first to admit that. They deal with life's challenges like any family, but the Osteen Girls' example is one worth following.

As women, wives, mothers and church leaders, they have demonstrated the influence a family can have in and through the various churches, ministries, missions, outreaches, books and networks they lead. The Osteen Girls were all gracious enough to conduct this interview with me via numerous emails and in spite of their busy travel schedules. I believe the result is a profile that is loaded with priceless wisdom. I have been personally inspired, challenged and touched through their lives and ministries and I hope you experience the same through reading these words.

The Osteen Girls have had ministry in their blood—since birth!

In 1959, their father and mother, John and Dodie Osteen founded Lakewood Church in a converted feed store. Together they raised five children (Paul, Lisa, Tamara, Joel, and April), all of whom are actively involved in leadership in the church today!

The most well known of the Osteens is the youngest son, Joel, who became the pastor of the Houston church in 1999 when their father passed away. While Joel's influence as an inspirational church leader is known around the world, he's not the only one who is fully immersed in leadership in the church—all of the Osteens are actively involved in ministry.

Paul is the oldest Osteen and after 17 years as a successful surgeon, he felt God's call to move to Houston and help at Lakewood Church in whatever capacity was needed. He provides oversight to all pastoral ministries and is one of the teaching pastors. He also spends several months a year doing missionary work in Africa—caring for patients, performing surgeries and ministering at local orphanages with his wife Jennifer and their children.

When it comes to the Osteen Girls – mother Dodie, daughters Lisa, Tamara, April and sisters-in-law Jennifer and Victoria (married to Joel) are blazing a trail for women, and God is using them in profound ways as they leave their own legacies that are deep and wide! Let's get to know the Osteen Girls:

DODIE:

Dodie Osteen married John Osteen in 1954 and together they had five children and founded Lakewood Church in Houston, Texas. They pastored the Lakewood congregation for 40 years and it was known as "The Oasis of Love in a Troubled World." Under their leadership, the church grew to a membership of nearly 6000. When John went home to be with the Lord in 1999, her youngest son Joel Osteen succeeded her husband as pastor.

Dodie is a member of the Greatest Generation (those born between 1922-1945), and for many of that generation, the role of women in the church was much more subdued and less visible. Dodie was a leader in faith when it was not as common for women to be leaders in the church. While Dodie was very supportive of her husband John, she was a leader and influencer in her own right when it came to living by faith and leaving that legacy to her children and others in the church. Dodie is most widely known for God's miraculous healing when she was diagnosed with liver cancer in 1981 and told she only had weeks to live. She was 48 years old at the time and didn't want to die. Her story of faith and healing has inspired her entire family and millions of others around the world, and the whole account is described in her book, *Healed of Cancer.*

Dodie's genuine warmth and compassion is one reason why people feel so loved and accepted when they enter the doors of Lakewood Church. After her dramatic healing from terminal cancer in 1981, God called her into a special ministry of prayer. Through that ministry of compassion, she has touched the lives of millions of people around the world. Dodie's influence as a woman in church leadership continues through her children.

When I asked her about the changes she's seen in the role of women in leadership in the church, Dodie said:

> *So many things have changed in the roles of women since I have been in the ministry. When John and I married in 1954, it was so different. We were in a denomination in which women were not seen frequently in the pulpit. Singing solos, teaching Sunday School, and making announcements were mainly what we did. When we had been married a few months, John said that God had spoken to his heart that I should make the announcements so the people could get acquainted with me. I did it and I shook when I did it! Now, anointed women of God preach, teach and even pastor. We've come a long way, baby!*

When it comes to her advice for women in the ministry today, Dodie said:

> *My advice for women in the ministry today is to walk in love and compassion just like Jesus did. Make everyone feel important, and that God's love and grace and forgiveness is for everyone. Follow the assignment that God has given you and minister to hurting people. People may criticize, but it is Jesus who has called us. Families should not be neglected, but loved and appreciated. Whatever you do, do it for the glory of the Lord Jesus, and He will bless you in abundance.*

LISA:

Lisa is the oldest daughter. Lisa Osteen Comes serves as an Executive Pastor of Lakewood Church. Born with a crippling birth defect that doctors said might keep her from walking, Lisa was miraculously healed as a child. In 1990, God spared her life when a pipe bomb sent thru the mail exploded in her lap. She is a Bible teacher and has traveled the world teaching God's Word and sharing the good news of Jesus Christ. Lisa is the author of *You Are Made for More*. She inspires people by telling them that no matter what they have been through or what they may face, God has a bright destiny for them to walk in. Sharing candidly about moving past crippling health issues, limiting labels, and unwanted divorce and broken dreams, she knows firsthand how God can restore our lives and make us stronger, wiser and more blessed than ever before.

I had the pleasure of hearing Lisa speak at a women's conference recently where she mentioned that as a divorced woman, she realized she had three strikes against her when it came to leadership in the church. She said, *"First: I am a woman. Second: I am divorced. Third: I am a woman."* Thankfully, she has pushed past those strikes and God is using her to hit home runs for Him everywhere she goes.

When it comes to women in the church, I asked Lisa, "What one thing would you say to women with a sense of destiny who feel called to lead and teach in the church?" Lisa responded:

> *Pursue your passion! Usually our desires are*

connected to our destiny so whatever God has put in your heart, pray about it, meditate on it and take any action steps you can today to see your dreams fulfilled. As a teen and young adult, I had a passion for God's Word. I would study and read books that helped me understand the Word better. I didn't know why then, but eventually I began to have a desire to preach, but I got scared thinking about it! I was not an outgoing person and literally hated having to make speeches in school.

After college, I started out working in the ministry as one of my dad's assistants, opening his mail and doing anything he needed. As I worked at Lakewood, I realized I had a passion for the Volunteer Ministries of the church and eventually became the Director of Ministries there for 16 years. During those years, I spoke to small groups and began to teach the Bible in our Bible classes and other areas.

One day, my dad asked me to fill the pulpit while he was away in India. I preached my first sermon on Sunday morning in 1985 with fear and trembling, and have been preaching ever since! I was blessed to have a father who recognized, encouraged, and empowered women in the ministry. He often said that the first woman preacher was the woman at the well, because Jesus commissioned her to go tell the good news of the Gospel.

As I look back on my life now, I can see how God was strategically preparing and directing my steps all along the way. I say all that to stress this truth— God prepares you for ministry daily, even though we can't see it now. Be faithful to do what you can today. Meet the needs of people you encounter today. Volunteer in your local church and allow God to prepare you and train you for the future. Ask God to mature you and open doors of opportunity for you to minister, and you will be amazed how God uses you.

I say often, "Do you want to know how to fulfill your God-given destiny?" You do it one day at a time— one faithful act of obedience, act of service, or time spent in prayer and the Word. These are daily decisions that catapult you into your full purpose. In reality, you are walking in your destiny today because God is directing your steps each and every day.

In response to my question on the biggest objection/criticism she's had to jump over as a woman in leadership in the church, Lisa said:

There are churches and people who believe women should not preach or pastor, and you may encounter this attitude from people at times. I really haven't encountered it too much because women ministers have been encouraged and trained at Lakewood for years. But at times, there are still people who want to give their opinion.

I encourage women to be themselves and don't apologize for who they are and for what God has called them to do. Be your feminine self and let God shine through you. It's not man versus woman; it's God using His children to labor together with Him in spreading the good news of the Gospel and helping hurting people.

Always respect and honor your leadership and pastor, as well as the men and women you work with. Don't let your emotions get in the way of your work relationships. Sometimes women can be easily offended and petty in their relationships with one another, but the more you strive for peace, the easier your job will be and the more favor and influence you will have.

One more thought, unless God has called you to minister specifically to women, don't limit yourself. I believe God wants to use women to minister to men, women, teens, and children. He has put gifts and anointing in you that will bless all people. You have greatness in you and don't let anyone tell you any different!

TAMARA:

Tamara Osteen Graff is a wife, mother of four and a Christian leader who is passionate about loving God, loving people and loving life. For over 25 years she has pastored alongside her husband, Jim, helping others to embrace the life of freedom and fulfillment that can only be found in God. Together, they founded Significant Church Network, a fellowship for church leaders in small to mid-sized towns throughout America. Through Significant Church, they host conferences and events where they encourage and remind pastors and their wives of their significant role in reaching people and influencing communities.

I've known Tamara for several years and it didn't take long to see how her compassion for people and her rich heritage of faith has enabled her to be a caring leader, a solid Bible teacher and a dynamic women's speaker. When it comes to women in leadership in the church, I asked Tamara, "What has been the biggest joy and/or challenge for you as a woman in ministry and leading a church with your husband?" Here's what Tamara said:

My greatest joy in ministry is seeing lives change for the better. About 25 years ago, my husband Jim and I joined arms with 200 dedicated believers in Victoria, Texas, to build a church together. Our goal was to create a culture where people could come to God just as they were, feeling loved as they learned to walk with Him.

Of course, every leader knows it's work to maintain that kind of culture as you grow through the different seasons of church life. But no matter how much effort it takes, it's always well worth it.

Now, every Sunday, there are several thousand in our city of 60,000, coming each week to worship, grow and serve God with their gifts. People are experiencing God's goodness in so many different ways, and I absolutely love seeing it happen. It has opened doors for us to serve in our schools, in our prisons, and among those who are hurting and in need all throughout our city.

Whether it's in our community, through Significant

Church, our network for pastors of churches in smaller areas, or through our efforts in reaching the unreached in India, it all fulfills the deepest parts of my heart. I love having a part in helping others live their best life in God.

I asked Tamara, "What one thing would you want to tell the next generation of women who feel called to leadership in the church?" Her answer is loaded with wisdom that comes from experience. She said:

Ministry can be both extremely rewarding and extremely challenging at times. Learning to balance the demands of ministry and people's expectations with personal and family life can be a struggle. It forces you to live with priorities in place and teaches you to say no to things that conflict with them. It's a constant effort to reevaluate your time, and to make sure you're giving the right amount of attention to the right things.

It can also be difficult to grow personally throughout different seasons of ministry. Oftentimes, I feel that just when I get something figured out, things change, and I get stretched all over again. I have learned though, that this constant stretching is actually a good thing because it keeps us dependent on God and upon His grace. Whether it's growing in skill, ability or in dealing with people, it takes a willingness to learn and embrace change for the future.

I would advise the next generation of women called to church leadership to focus on ministering from the inside out. Give your attention first to your marriage and family, and then let your ministry develop from there.

So many times we feel the pressure to take on responsibilities within the church, to "be this" and "do that," when the reality is that our greatest responsibility and reward is in managing our own home well.

When you think about it, our marriage is the glue that holds everything else together. If that's not right, things will be negatively affected down the road. Most of us in ministry marry strong leaders and visionaries. They shoulder a lot of responsibility and are continually giving of themselves. They often come home emotionally spent and needing to be refreshed. The wife can and needs to be her husband's most trusted friend, his biggest fan and loudest cheerleader. Her respect, love and encouragement means more to him than anyone else's.

I believe if we can work toward building and maintaining a strong marriage, it will produce not only a healthy family but also a healthy ministry. I'm not saying not to do anything in the church; what I am saying is to make sure your influence is felt first and foremost within your own home.

Women can be gifted leaders, communicators and influencers, and there's no limit to the way God can use them. Still, I am strongly convinced that a woman's greatest legacy comes from ministering well from the inside out.

APRIL:

April Osteen Simons is the wife of the Rev. Gary Simons, pastor of the High Point Church in Arlington, Texas. She believes that pastors' wives have to learn to be themselves and not try to live up to a "perfect" image. She learned that growing up in Houston watching her mother, Dodie Osteen, and her father, the late Rev. John Osteen, founder of Lakewood Church. *"I think my mother and father were the greatest people in the world, and I learned a lot from them,"* she said. *"The biggest thing they taught me was to be real. They lived their lives, not perfectly, but they were the same people on the platform that they were at home."* According to Dodie, *"Lisa was the youngest Osteen and she always said she was our favorite!"*

April said she grew up wanting to be a pastor's wife. But she has had struggles, too. *"Sometimes it's difficult not being the people you are expected to be,"* Simons said. *"I think a lot of people think a pastor's wife doesn't go through hard times, but that's just a fallacy."*

These days April believes God is doing great things through women in the church and when asked what she would say to women about balancing/juggling their calling to lead in the church with their roles as wife and mom, she said:

> *I would say to keep the main thing the main thing. To me, my marriage and family always come first. Pastoring can be a 24/7 job if we allow it. If we're not careful, we can "take on" the issues of the church; including the people in the church.*

There'll come a time when you have to leave it at the office and go to your greatest mission field, which is your home. Too many times, we allow our own households to suffer for the sake of ministry. This is entirely out of balance.

What good are we if, in the end, we have a great ministry, but our home has fallen apart? I don't want my kids and husband to ever say they were second choice. I want to lay my head on the pillow at night knowing that I have my priorities straight. I believe God gives us wisdom to know when we're out of balance.

We MUST do our part to heed that still, small voice and do what we know needs to be done...even if a few people are disappointed.

In response to the question of what her greatest challenge as a woman in ministry was, April said:

I believe the greatest challenge we, as women, face is keeping the balance. I believe if God calls us to do something, then He gives us the grace to accomplish it. And He gives us this grace without us having to sacrifice our marriage or family.

I've been in a ministry family all of my life. I have seen a lot. I've seen amazing Christian families suffer for the sake of "ministry." I've seen pastors' kids feel overlooked and ignored. I've seen the hurt all in the name of "ministry." I've seen families so out of balance that it was shocking to me even as a child. I wanted to say, "Can't you see what you're doing to your family?"

It was foreign to me because my parents were far from perfect, but were such great role models. They treated us like we mattered. They spent time with us. They pastored a great church and cared about people, and yet they had time for us. We were priorities in their lives. My dad even put on the calendar every week, "Family Day." The staff knew not to mess with that day...changing it was not an option! And because of this, we loved and admired what my parents did for a living. They were the real deal. They didn't just preach it...they lived it.

I made a decision when I had my own family that, to the best of my ability, I would strive to keep my life in balance so that my family is number one. I want them to know that I will drop everything for them. This helps me stay in check. It helps me keep my balance. I don't always succeed, but I know what my goal is. And when I fail, God's grace helps me get back in balance. No family is perfect. But what makes life perfect is a family that knows they are loved, adored and a priority.

Know your limits. Know when to say, "no." Stop thinking you have to do it all. Keep boundaries. And remember...nothing is more important than those people in your house who belong to you...with all of their messes and laundry and shoes all over the house...they're yours. Make sure they get the best of you and not the leftover, beaten down, stressed out version of you.

You get one shot at this thing called life. Make sure it counts!

JENNIFER:

Jennifer Osteen is married to Paul, the oldest Osteen son, a general surgeon who also serves in pastoral and teaching ministries at Lakewood Church. Together, Paul and Jennifer have four children.

Jennifer is a nurse and has seen God use her to care for the sick in the States and overseas on various missions trips—particularly to Africa (primarily Kenya and Zambia) where she and her children often help Paul in caring for patients, performing surgeries and ministering at mission hospitals and local orphanages.

As a Christian woman and leader, she is not a fan of public speaking, but is willing to do it on her bravest days. Her first love is small groups and connecting with women of all ages face to face.

In addition to being a devoted wife and mother, Jennifer is a great writer and hosts a blog, "The Perfectly Imperfect Messy Girl's Journey," where she describes herself as a recovering perfectionist, mom-to-four, drinker of too much Diet Dr. Pepper, laundry-conqueror, kitchen-dweller, Africa-lover and Jesus-worshipper. She recently wrote this funny blog describing her experience in public speaking.

Speaking is a beast. Following my experienced, very eloquent husband felt like facing Godzilla. I've spoken in front of people maybe three times in the last 14 years that we have been in ministry. The last time was SO long ago I completely forgot the way your heart beats hard like it may pop out of your chest and the intense dry mouth that the Pacific Ocean couldn't quench. Not to mention the nerve-calming (yet super distracting) way I tend to move around on stage like I have Restless Leg Syndrome. I was so relieved when my little part was over, but I couldn't recall one word I said. I wasn't sure if I had killed Godzilla or if I'd been been devoured. My prayer was that somehow I hadn't irreparably scarred my teenagers by getting up in front of their "hip" crowd looking odd, quirky and unconvincingly hip. My sweet daughter asked me afterward why I'd even agree to speak if it brought me that close to a nervous breakdown. Good question. Very good question. I promise I repeatedly asked myself the same question after the service. Here's why I said yes, bought a new pair of skinny jeans and agreed to try something that could potentially embarrass me in front of hundreds of cool people— because I'm fighting the need to be perfect and to be seen as perfect. (And let me tell you, I cleared that one up!)

She loves leading small groups and offers the women she leads at Lakewood Church a lifetime of wisdom. When asked about her advice to women who feel called to ministry or leadership in the church, but who struggle with insecurities, she had this to say:

Doubt, fear, comparison and insecurities have held women back for too long from taking their rightful place serving in the church. It held me back for far too long. When I was growing up, I perceived my pastor's wife and other women in ministry as perfect. I assumed they had it all together, without a problem in the world. What that did was create a false measuring stick for me that I'd never measure up to on my best day. On top of that, I had childhood wounds and hurts that dogged my self-esteem.

I thank God for bringing down those misconceptions in my mind by giving me mentors and friends in ministry through the years who were transparent and honest about their lives. Watching God use these women in powerful ways, despite their own self doubt, inspired me. Really, at the end of the day, we are all alike. I don't know a single WOMAN who doesn't struggle with something.

God's not looking for a perfect daughter. He's looking for a brave daughter, an available daughter, a passionate and devoted daughter, but not a perfect one.

My advice would be: Be brave! Don't waste another minute. God wants to use your strengths and gifts to help others and strengthen the body of Christ. He even wants to use your weaknesses and fears. There's nothing good or bad in your past, present or future that can't bring God glory, if you'll let it. The enemy will use our insecurities to keep us idle and sidelined, but God wants us in the game—all of us! God's not tripped up by our insecurities, so we shouldn't be either.

I find the more transparent and honest I am about the hard and messy parts of my life, the more God's grace becomes real and tangible to other women. Be brave enough to step out and up!

When asked, "What would you say to the next generation of women who feel a call to serve God in the and through the church," she said,

I have three teenage daughters and meet regularly with a group of young women from our church. Several of these are already in ministry in some capacity. I remind them all the time that there are seasons to every woman's life. Never forsake your husband or children for another (seemingly more glamorous or important) ministry. Your family should always be your number one place of service.

I'd never, ever go back and change those "hidden years" of raising my children, because I knew that season would only last for a certain amount of time and I could never redo those years. Be faithful in the place that God has you now, whether that's home with toddlers or teaching a Bible study in your church. When you have been consistent and faithful where you are, and that season ends, you can be sure God has something else in store. To my daughters and other young girls feeling a desire to serve I'd say you are never too young and when you say, 'God use me,' He will! Volunteer—get involved—you have something to offer that is uniquely yours! Follow your passions and discover your gifts and then let God show you where they intersect for His glory.

VICTORIA:

Victoria is a mother of two and co-pastor of Lakewood Church, as well as a passionate and active leader with a global ministry. Victoria's teaching and exhortation are not only an important part of each Lakewood service, but also extremely popular outside the church, as well, reaching more than 38 million people weekly through her website and social media outlets. As a high profile pastor's wife, New York Times bestselling author, women's ministry leader and mother of two, she understands the pressures women face these days and is an inspiration and mentor to women everywhere. She believes that inside every woman lies a person of strength and beauty with unique gifts and God-given talents to make a significant impact on their families and their community. This passion led her to found the Women's Ministry at Lakewood designed to strengthen and improve the lives of married, single and professional women by inspiring them to discover their gifts and develop them to their fullest potential. Her book, *Love Your Life: Living Happy, Healthy and Whole,* has encouraged today's busy modern women with a plan to help them embrace joy and live life to the fullest!

When I asked Victoria, "How do you identify/balance your own identity as a wife, mom, leader and teacher in the church while supporting a very high profile husband/pastor," she said:

> *I believe one of the greatest ways to keep yourself strong and growing is to understand your value and your significance, not only in the lives of the people around you, but in the world as well. Where*

I am today is not where I started. But I have always believed that my life would make a difference, and that God places great value, significance and importance on my life. When I am doing what I'm called to do, it is like the rippling effect of throwing a stone in the water. In a similar way, my life "ripples out" and has influence on those around me.

Whether I am in the role of a wife, mother or pastor, I have great worth and great responsibility. Does that mean I feel strong and valuable every day? No! But it isn't the way I feel that matters, it's what I know and believe about myself. Feelings come and go, but what you believe about yourself is based on what you are feeding your mind every day. Wrong thoughts and wrong mindsets will distort your sense of value and worth, and cause you to fall short of your potential. I stay in the habit of speaking faith filled words over my life because I believe a healthy self-image will bring balance and worth to all those around me.

On the topic of what advice she would give her daughter and the next generation of women who feel called to do what she is doing—that is, lead a church in partnership with her husband—she answered with wisdom that every young girl needs to hear:

When I was a young girl, I remember I asked the Lord to give me a husband who would help strengthen my faith, not one I would have to drag along with me. What I meant was I wanted someone who had a heart for God completely, and showed it in his actions. One piece of advice that I give my daughter is to do what I did: study the important things in your potential husband long before you say, "Yes." I studied Joel before we were married, noticing things like his work ethic, how he treated his family (especially his mother), and how he spoke about his friends. I observed his faith in action, and I loved his joy.

The second piece of advice I give my daughter is to always remember that you and your husband are a team. One thing I can say, after 27 years of marriage, is that Joel and I have always been of one mind and one mission —a team. Joel and I built houses together when we were young, we built a TV station a few years later, and today we are working together building a global ministry. When you are of one mission and are dedicated to the other's success, you will be successful as a team.

Finally, I tell my daughter and everyone else, the greatest thing Joel and I have learned is to respect one another. We don't always agree on everything, but we agree to disagree respectfully. The truth is we only respect what we value, so we must never allow our words to devalue one another. It is important to remind ourselves that God brought us together to do great things. I have always valued my husband and spoken success over him, and I would urge anyone to do the same.

As you can see, wisdom and the heritage of faith is alive and well in the Osteen Girls, as they have discovered their own unique gifts and are fulfilling their God-given purposes as wives, mothers and leaders in and through the church!

You can connect with the Osteen Girls at:

Dodie Osteen: www.lakewoodchurch.com

Lisa Osteen Comes: www.lisacomes.com

Tamara Osteen Graff: www.myffc.com

April Osteen Simmons: www.highpointchurch.com

Jennifer Osteen: www.jenniferosteen.com

Victoria Osteen: www.victoriaosteen.com

Chapter 3

THOSE CONTROVERSIAL SCRIPTURES ABOUT WOMEN

Women must be silent in the church! Women must not speak. Women cannot teach men.

All women must be submissive to all men. The Bible says so!

Does it?

I received this email a few years ago:

> *Hi Beth, my husband works with two women who came to church and heard you preach last Sunday. They have asked my husband how he could go to a church that has a woman preaching when the Bible teaches that it is wrong. They did not give Scripture to support this, but I assume they might be referring to I Corinthians 14:34-35 and/or I Timothy 2:11-15. I know that you have taught on this before, however we both want to be reminded of that teaching to share with people who ask such questions.*

This email was from a great couple who has grown in our church and been used of God to serve others. I understood the difficulty they faced as they were challenged by her husband's coworkers. Let's look at the verses of Scripture she mentioned, but first can we talk about gnats and camels?

HAVE WE BEEN STRAINING AT A GNAT?

Is it possible that on a controversial topic like this, we have been straining at a gnat and missing the larger picture, as well as the heart of God? As we begin this study, it might be helpful to take off any "biased" glasses we may be wearing. Sometimes, we can become so focused on one particular verse or a train of thought that we are prejudiced in our understanding and miss the larger picture, and the whole counsel of God's Word. With that in mind, I want to encourage you to open your heart afresh to the Lord and His Spirit as we explore His Word.

Jesus was painfully blunt with the religious nit-picking mentality of His day.

> *"Woe to you, scribes and Pharisees, hypocrites! For you pay tithe of mint and anise and cummin, and have neglected the weightier matters of the law: justice and mercy and faith. These you ought to have done, without leaving the others undone.* **Blind guides, who strain out a gnat and swallow a camel!***" (Matthew 23:23-24, NKJV, emphasis mine).*

Jesus himself faced the rejection and controversy that came from those who were presumptuous in their understanding of the Word, their facts and His calling. The Pharisees thought they were right about the Messiah and their interpretation of the scriptures, but they were wrong. They didn't rightly divide the Word. Their dogmatic focus on the "gnat" caused them to miss the "camel"—the Messiah in their midst!

Don't major on the minors.

It wasn't just the Pharisees, there were many others who quoted the scriptures about the Christ with authority, but they were wrong in their interpretation.

> *"Therefore many from the crowd, when they heard this saying, said, 'Truly this is the Prophet.' Others said, 'This is the Christ.' But some said, 'Will the Christ come out of Galilee? Has not the Scripture said that the Christ comes from the seed of David and from the town of Bethlehem, where David was?' So there was a division among the people because of Him"* (John 7:40-43, NKJV).

They knew the scripture and quoted it boldly, yet they were mistaken about its meaning and they missed the visitation of God! They didn't recognize Jesus or His role in the world. It was the snare of spiritual pride. As a result, they rejected Jesus and missed out on all of the benefits the Father sent Him to bring to them—all because of their misunderstanding of the Word. How sad it that?

If we are not careful, we can fall into the same trap and become so dogmatic in our application of one or two verses that mention the role of women in the church, that we may miss the larger picture and whole counsel of the Word on this topic. Is it possible that someone could reject a woman whom God has gifted with a preaching or leadership gift and miss out on the benefits the Lord could have brought into their lives through her ministry?

THE "LETTER"OR THE "SPIRIT"?

Perhaps the Apostle Paul knew something about this type of thinking when he wrote about the difference between "the letter" and "the Spirit" as it related to God's Word and his calling to the ministry.

> *"Not that we are competent in ourselves to claim anything for ourselves, but our competence comes from God. He has made us competent as ministers of a new covenant—not of the letter but of the Spirit; for **the letter kills, but the Spirit gives life**"* (2 Corinthians 3:5-6, NIV, emphasis mine).

We don't want to be the type of people who isolate one or two verses and get snared by the "letter of the law," while missing the "spirit of the law." What is the Spirit saying to us through God's Word regarding the role of women in the church? The Bible tells us to study the Word and compare spiritual things with spiritual.

> *Study and be eager and do your utmost to present yourself to God approved (tested by trial), a workman who has no cause to be ashamed, **correctly analyzing and accurately dividing [rightly handling and skillfully teaching] the Word of Truth** (2 Timothy 2:15, AMP, emphasis mine).*

*"But as it is written: 'Eye has not seen, nor ear heard, nor have entered into the heart of man the things which God has prepared for those who love Him.' But God has revealed them to us through His Spirit. For the Spirit searches all things, yes, the deep things of God. For what man knows the things of a man except the spirit of the man which is in him? Even so no one knows the things of God except the Spirit of God. Now we have received, not the spirit of the world, but the Spirit who is from God, that we might know the things that have been freely given to us by God. **These things we also speak, not in words which man's wisdom teaches but which the Holy Spirit teaches, comparing spiritual things with spiritual.** But the natural man does not receive the things of the Spirit of God, for they are foolishness to him; nor can he know them, because they are spiritually discerned. But he who is spiritual judges all things, yet he himself is rightly judged by no one. For 'who has known the mind of the Lord that he may instruct Him?' But we have the mind of Christ"* (1 Corinthians 2:9-16, NKJV, emphasis mine).

SILENT AND SUBSERVIENT?

Let's dive in and take a look at the main "controversial" passages that are often cited to support the theological position that women must be silent and subservient in church. How do we rightly divide these verses?

Controversial Verse #1

The Apostle Paul wrote these words. *"**Let your women keep**

silent in the churches, for they are not permitted to speak; but *they are to be submissive, as the law also says. And if they want to learn something, let them ask their own husbands at home; for it is shameful for women to speak in church"* (1 Corinthians 14:34-35, NKJV, emphasis mine).

Controversial Verse #2

*"Let a woman learn in silence with all submission. And **I do not permit a woman to teach or to have authority over a man, but to be in silence**. For Adam was formed first, then Eve. And Adam was not deceived, but the woman being deceived, fell into transgression. Nevertheless she will be saved in childbearing if they continue in faith, love, and holiness, with self-control"* (1 Timothy 2:11-15, NKJV, emphasis mine).

It sure looks like these verses are telling women they cannot teach, preach, or lead in the church—period! At first glance, it's clear isn't it? Women must be silent in the church. Women are not allowed to speak, teach, or carry a leadership role over the men, right?

Or. . . maybe not.

Let's take a moment to be certain we are rightly dividing the Word of truth by asking some questions and comparing spiritual things with spiritual.

Let's start by talking about the "silence" issue. If women are to be silent—not speaking, teaching, preaching, or leading—

how do we explain the numerous other passages of Scripture where God anoints women to speak, prophesy, preach, proclaim and edify the church?

Contradictory Verse #1

"And it shall come to pass in the last days, saith God, **I will pour out my Spirit upon all flesh: and your sons and your daughters shall prophesy,** *and your young men shall see visions, and your old men shall dream dreams:* **And on my servants and on my handmaidens I will pour out in those days of my Spirit; and they shall prophesy"** (Acts 2:17-18, emphasis mine).

God promises to pour out His Spirit on all flesh in the last days, including men and women!

Contradictory Verse #2

The Apostle Paul wrote, *"But* **every woman who prays or prophesies** *with her head uncovered dishonors her head, for that is one and the same as if her head were shaved"* (1 Corinthians 11:5, NKJV, emphasis mine).

Contradictory Verse #3

We see Philip, the evangelist's four daughters prophesying.

"... Philip the evangelist ... had **four daughters,** *virgins, which* **did prophesy"** (Acts 21:8-9, emphasis mine).

It's clear from these Scriptures that women, daughters and handmaidens will *not* be silent, but will prophesy. What does it mean to prophesy and where does prophesy take place? Let's look at the definition for "prophesy" as revealed in 1 Corinthians.

> *"But he who **prophesies speaks edification and exhortation and comfort** to men . . . he who **prophesies edifies the church** . . ."* (1 Corinthians 14:3-4, NKJV, emphasis mine).

The first thing we see is that *"he who prophesies speaks"* Speaking is the exact opposite of being silent. Women who prophesy will speak. What will they speak? This verse tells us that prophesy is comprised of words spoken to edify, exhort, and comfort others.

To prophesy, according to Vine's Expository Dictionary, means, "telling forth the divine counsels."[1] Thayer's Greek Lexicon tells us that to prophesy means, "to teach, refute, reprove, admonish, and comfort."[2]

Adam Clarke's Commentary says, "The word prophesy is not to be understood here as implying the knowledge and discovery of future events; but signifies to teach and proclaim the great truths of God, especially those which concerned redemption by Jesus Christ."[3]

The word "prophesy," simply put, is inspired speaking, preaching, proclaiming, and teaching which edifies, exhorts and comforts.

Another thing we notice from this verse in 1 Corinthians 14 is that *"he who prophesies edifies the church."* That means if a woman is to prophesy, she would be speaking words that edify the church.

If women—daughters and handmaidens—are supposed to prophesy to edify the church, but yet at the same time be silent in the church, how is this possible? Obviously, it isn't. Can you see the incongruences? The Bible states as a matter of fact and common practice that women (and men) would prophesy—preach, teach, and speak to the church for the purpose of edification, exhortation, and comfort.

Again, Adam Clarke's Commentary summarizes the idea of men and women prophesying and emphasizes that whatever the definition of prophesying is—as it relates to a man—it has to have the exact same meaning in respect to a woman.

> *"Whatever may be the meaning of praying and prophesying, in respect to the man, they have precisely the same meaning in respect to the woman. So that some women at least, as well as some men, might speak to others to edification, and exhortation, and comfort. And this kind of prophesying or teaching was predicted by Joel, Joel 2:28, and referred to by Peter, Acts 2:17."[4]*

DOES THE BIBLE CONTRADICT ITSELF?

How do these facts square with the verses stating that women must be silent in the church? To be "silent in the church" would clearly be the opposite of "prophesying in the church."

Is the Bible contradicting itself with these statements?

"Women must keep silent in the church . . ."

"Women are not permitted to teach . . ."

"In the last days I will pour out my Spirit and your sons and daughters will prophesy . . ."

"But every woman who prays or prophesies..."

"You may all prophesy..."

On one hand, we see two verses that tell us women must be silent in the church. On the other hand, we see many other verses that tell us God has poured out His Spirit on daughters and handmaidens, and these same women are to prophesy—teach, preach, and proclaim to edify the church.

Of course, the Bible does not contradict itself.

God is not confused on the subject.

A CULTURAL ISSUE OR A THEOLOGICAL ISSUE?

Let's take a closer look at these passages. Just what did the Apostle Paul mean when he wrote about "women," "silence" and "the church?"

*"**Let your women keep silence in the churches**: for it is not permitted unto them to speak; but they are commanded to be under obedience as also saith the law. And if they will learn any thing, let them ask their husbands at home: for **it is a shame***

for women to speak in the church" (1 Corinthians 14:34-35, emphasis mine).

"Let the woman learn in silence *with all subjection. But I* **suffer not a woman to teach,** *nor to usurp authority over the man,* **but to be in silence"** (1 Timothy 2:11-12, emphasis mine).

Scholars tell us from a study on church culture and history that Paul's phrase, "women keep silence in the churches," is a reference to a cultural problem they were having in the early church.

There are several views on how this played out in history. One common explanation is that it was customary in the synagogue during New Testament times for the women to sit on one side of the building and the men to sit on the opposite side. It was culturally acceptable for a man to interrupt the speaker with his questions; however, it was not culturally acceptable for a woman to do so. As a result, during the service, if a woman had a question about something she did not understand, she would blurt out her question to her husband across the room and disrupt the speaker and the service. Paul admonished them for this and said that women must be silent in the church and if they wanted to learn the answers to their questions, they must ask their own husbands at home.

The culture of the early church did not regard women very highly. The Jewish Talmud said, *"Out of respect to the congregation, a woman should not herself read in the law. It is a shame for a woman to let her voice be heard among men. The voice of a woman is filthy nakedness."* [5]

Origen (A.D. 185-254), the early church father said, *"Men should not sit and listen to a woman . . . even if she says admirable things, or even saintly things, that is of little consequence, since they came from the mouth of a woman."*[6]

Jerome (A.D. 342-420), an early church father and well-known Biblical scholar and translator of the Bible into Latin (the Vulgate) had a simple view of women. To him *"woman is the root of all evil."*[7]

It wasn't just the early church fathers who spoke ill of women, even Martin Luther spoke as one affected by the culture, rather than the heart of Jesus when he said, *"If women get tired and die of [child] bearing, there is no harm in that; let them die as long as they bear; they are made for that."* He also said, *"Woman must neither begin nor complete anything without man: Where he is, there she must be, and bend before him as before a master, whom she shall fear and to whom she shall be subject and obedient."* [8]

Of course, animosity towards women is not new. It began in the Garden of Eden. Genesis 3:15 describes the intense war between Satan and women, *"And I will put enmity between you and the woman, and between your seed and her Seed; He shall bruise your head, and you shall bruise His heel"* (NKJV). Satan has oppressed women for centuries because he realized that it was the Seed of the woman that would destroy him. Jesus Christ the Redeemer would come from the Seed of a woman and Satan wasn't happy about it. When Jesus came on the scene, He crushed Satan's head! He redeemed mankind from sin and death and set men and women totally free!

As a result, Jesus broke the ongoing oppression between Satan and women. We have been redeemed from the curse! No other religion has given dignity and freedom to women like Jesus and Christianity. That is why it is so heartbreaking to see people, in the Name of Christ, siding in with Satan's enmity against women, rather than siding in with Jesus and the freedom and redemption He brought to men and women.

What do other scholars say about the enmity against women and their role in the church?

Adam Clarke's Commentary tells us regarding 1 Corinthians 14:34:

> *This was a Jewish ordinance; women were not permitted to teach in the assemblies, or even to ask questions. The rabbis taught that "a woman should know nothing but the use of her distaff." And the sayings of Rabbi Eliezer, as delivered, Bammidbar Rabba, sec. 9, fol. 204, are both worthy of remark and of execration; they are these: "Let the words of the law be burned, rather than that they should be delivered to women." This was their condition till the time of the Gospel, when, according to the prediction of Joel, the Spirit of God was to be poured out on the women as well as the men, that they might prophesy, i.e. teach. And that they did prophesy or teach is evident from what the apostle says, 1 Corinthians 11:5, where he lays down rules to regulate this part of their conduct while ministering*

in the church. . . . It is evident from the context that the apostle refers here to asking questions, and what we call dictating in the assemblies. It was permitted to any man to ask questions, to object, altercate, attempt to refute, etc., in the synagogue; but this liberty was not allowed to any woman. St. Paul confirms this in reference also to the Christian Church; he orders them to keep silence; and, if they wished to learn anything, let them inquire of their husbands at home; because it was perfectly indecorous for women to be contending with men in public assemblies, on points of doctrine, cases of conscience, etc. But this by no means intimated that when a woman received any particular influence from God to enable her to teach, that she was not to obey that influence; on the contrary, she was to obey it, and the apostle lays down directions in 1 Corinthians chapter 11 for regulating her personal appearance when thus employed.[9]

In reference to Paul's comments about women learning in silence and not usurping authority over men, the International Standard Bible Encyclopedia says . . .

. . . possibly because some women had been offensively forward in 'usurping authority over the man' (1 Timothy 2:12). Even though he bases his argument for woman's keeping silence in public worship on Adam's priority of creation and her priority in transgression (1 Timothy 2:13-14), modern scholarship unhesitatingly affirms that his prohibition was applicable only to the peculiar conditions of his own time. Her culture, grace, scholarship, ability, religious devotion and spiritual enduement make it evident that she is often as truly

called of God to public address and instruction as man. It is evident in the New Testament and in the writings of the Apostolic Fathers that women, through the agency of two ecclesiastical orders, were assigned official duties in the conduct and ministrations of the early church.[10]

During the Old and New Testament times, there were distinct separations between men and women in daily life and culture. These cultural norms have changed in many parts of the world these days, but perhaps the church has not recognized these cultural changes.

THE SISTERS ARE RIGHT!

As we wrap up this chapter, I want to draw your attention to a passage of Scripture you don't hear much about in Numbers 27:1-7. Zelophehad and his five daughters were alive and a part of Israel's exodus from Egypt and the journey to the Promised Land. Here's the story:

> *"Then came the daughters of Zelophehad the son of Hepher, the son of Gilead, the son of Machir, the son of Manasseh, from the families of Manasseh the son of Joseph; and these were the names of his daughters: Mahlah, Noah, Hoglah, Milcah, and Tirzah. And they stood before Moses, before Eleazar the priest, and before the leaders and all the congregation, by the doorway of the tabernacle of meeting, saying: 'Our father died in the wilderness; but he was not in the company of those who gathered together against the LORD, in company with Korah, but he died in his own sin; and*

he had no sons. Why should the name of our father be removed from among his family because he had no son? Give us a possession among our father's brothers.' So Moses brought their case before the LORD. And the LORD spoke to Moses, saying: 'The daughters of Zelophehad speak what is right; you shall surely give them a possession of inheritance among their father's brothers, and cause the inheritance of their father to pass to them...'"

There are several important truths embedded in this passage. In Bible times, when it came to the laws of inheritance—history and tradition tell us that the male children, especially the first born, were the ones to be heirs of any property rights a father left his children. In Zelophehad's case, he died, but he did not have any sons. The five sisters felt they should be given the rights to their father's property; otherwise their father's name and legacy would be gone forever. They presented their case to Moses and Moses brought their case before the Lord. According to the letter of the law, these sisters would have to live without an inheritance of property; however, according to the spirit of the law—listen to God's response: *"The daughters of Zelophehad speak what is right..."*

I love that! God obviously sees the bigger picture in every situation—He operates from a position of truth and grace—and He agreed with the sisters! God was willing to hear their case. He recognized the common sense, logic, fairness and justice in what the girls presented and He said, *"The sisters are right!"* and He gave them their inheritance.

Those five sisters broke through some "granite tablet

ceilings" that day! I don't know about you, but that whole story encourages me and tells me a lot about the heart of God.

Girls, be encouraged!

I hope through this chapter you are beginning to see this topic in a fresh new light. I know this subject has been examined, written about and debated by people who are much more experienced and scholarly than me, but is it possible that we have been straining at a gnat and misunderstood the spirit of these passages? Is it conceivable that we have allowed a few verses that are culturally based (and incongruent with other scriptures) to be the plumb line for the destiny of millions of women? As a result, how many ladies have been paralyzed and robbed of a large part of their destiny? How much has the world and Body of Christ lost by adherence to these ways of thinking? How many women with a distinct calling from God to teach, a passion to preach, and an anointing to lead have lived and died frustrated and unfulfilled in their God-given purpose?

Let's look at another facet of this subject that has been the source of misunderstanding.

CHAPTER 4

CAN WOMEN TEACH MEN?

*O*k, maybe women can teach, preach and prophesy but . . . what about women teaching men? Leading men? Being a pastor? Doesn't the Bible teach against that? Isn't a woman supposed to be covered by a man? Aren't women the weaker sex and created to be inferior and subservient to men?

Are all women of a lesser rank than all men? Should all women, as a gender, be submissive to all men, as a gender?

Let's just start World War III, eh?

In some religious circles, it is taught that women in general, should be submissive to men in general. Is that God's view? The Apostle Paul addressed this by saying, *"There is neither Jew nor Greek, slave nor free, **male nor female**, for you are all one in Christ Jesus"* (Galatians 3:28, NIV, emphasis mine). In Christ, men and women are equal—but what does that mean?

Let's look at a few different scenarios: daily living relationships, marriage relationships and church relationships.

In daily relationships, the rule of thumb for all New Testament believers is equality and a command to walk in the law of love. Christian men and women are to love one another, prefer one another and submit to one another in love (John 13:34, Romans 12:10, Ephesians 5:21).

In marriage relationships, God has established certain roles and responsibilities for men and for women. In the area of spiritual authority, the Bible is clear about the relationship between husbands and wives. Husbands are to love their own wives as Christ loves the Church (Ephesians 5:25) and women are to be submitted to their own husbands as to Christ (1 Peter 3:5). In marriage, the relationship between the husband and wife should not be a war between a dictator husband and his inferior or insubordinate wife, but should be one that mirrors the loving and submissive relationship we have with the Lord Jesus Christ. The Amplified Bible brings out the mutual spirit of love and submission in this relationship:

> *"Be subject to one another out of reverence for Christ (the Messiah, the Anointed One). Wives, be subject (be submissive and adapt yourselves) to your own husbands as [a service] to the Lord ... Husbands, love your wives, as Christ loved the church and gave Himself up for her ... Even so husbands should love their wives as [being in a sense] their own bodies. He who loves his own wife loves himself. For no man ever hated his own flesh, but nourishes and carefully protects and cherishes it, as Christ does the church ... However, let each man of you [without exception] love his wife as [being in a sense] his very own self; and let the wife see that she respects and reverences her husband that she notices him, regards him, honors him, prefers him, venerates, and esteems*

him; and that she defers to him, praises him, and loves and admires him exceedingly]" (Ephesians 5:21-22, 25, 28-29, 33, AMP).

In church relationships, there are numerous views on the roles of men and women. Let's look at various scenarios.

DIFFERENT RULES

In certain pockets of Christianity, women—as a gender—are expected to be submissive to all of the male gender. In other words, some believe that in God's eyes, women are completely under the authority of men. The result is that women are only allowed to teach or lead other women. An older woman is encouraged to teach the younger woman, as the Scripture says, but she is not allowed to teach or lead the men.

In other segments of the church world, a woman may teach or lead young boys and young men, but she may not teach or lead adult men. Of course the question arises, when does a boy or young man actually become a man? When he turns 18? When he's married? How old does the man have to be before a woman is forbidden to teach or lead him?

In some church circles, women are allowed to teach and lead men on the mission field—in the uttermost parts of the earth—where mosquitoes are as big as helicopters and mud huts and snake filets are as good as it gets, but they are not allowed to do so in America. Why the inconsistent standards? Is gender prejudice in the church simply an American issue?

J. Lee Grady, Christian leader and author of *10 Lies the Church Tells Women*, shares the story of his involvement with a campus ministry in the 1980's, and their view on inviting a woman to be a speaker at the conference for Christian college students. It would be funny, if it weren't so sad. He writes:

> *Over the years I've heard countless arguments used to restrict women from preaching or leading churches. When I was involved with a charismatic campus ministry in the 1980's, the top directors gathered on one occasion to decide what speakers to invite to a conference for Christian college students.*
>
> *When someone suggested they invite a well-known woman speaker this was the response:*
>
> *The president of the campus group said, "It will be OK if she 'shares' the Word, but she can't preach. Women share." The idea was that if women are put in a place of public ministry and are asked to speak, they must do it meekly (or sheepishly) to somehow demonstrate that they are not being forceful in the presence of men. How ridiculous! Perhaps the men are afraid that the women will preach better?* [1]

In many churches, a woman may sing a song that teaches Bible truths in front of men; but if she is not singing her message, a woman may not teach by speaking Bible truths to men in the form of a sermon or Bible study. Where is the line? A woman is allowed to sing, but she must not speak? A woman may hum or sing a message from God's Word, but she may not teach, preach or speak a message from the Bible in a way that does not include a melody? In his book, J. Lee Grady tells the story about one church that required the woman who was singing to turn her back on the audience and sing while facing the wall, so she did not violate scriptures. Can you see how ridiculous "straining the gnat" becomes? Do these examples sound like "the letter of the law" or "the Spirit of the law"?

WOMEN VERSUS WIVES

Let's again look at the two passages we've already reviewed and further define our terms.

*"Let a woman learn in silence with all submission. And **I do not permit a woman to teach or to have authority over a man, but to be in silence.** For Adam was formed first, then Eve. And Adam was not deceived, but the woman being deceived, fell into transgression. Nevertheless **she will be saved in childbearing** if they continue in faith, love, and holiness, with self-control"* (1 Timothy 2:11-15, NKJV, emphasis mine).

Notice, the passage says, *"And I do not permit a woman to teach or to have authority over a man, but to be in silence."* What type of woman is not allowed to teach or have authority over a man? All women? Married women? What type of men? All men? Married men?

One sentence in this passage tells us just exactly whom the Apostle Paul was referring to. He is talking about married women and their husbands. Married women should not have authority over their husbands. He is not talking about all women; he is talking about married women. How do we know?

It's clear that he is talking about married women because he says this woman *"will be saved in childbearing."* Who bears children? All women? Single women? No. Married women! The context of this passage is clearly speaking to the role of married women and married men. That is, this passage is talking about the role of husbands and wives.

The context of this passage is that wives should *not* teach or have authority over their own husbands, not that women are not allowed to teach or lead men, in general. This makes sense as it is congruent with the rest of the Bible and the teaching on the role of husbands and wives.

As we dig a little deeper into this passage, we find that the words "woman" and "man" are the Greek words *gune* and *aner,* which are often translated as "wife" and "husband," respectively.[2] Therefore, in context, this verse could easily be read, *"I do not permit a wife to teach or to have authority over the husband, but to be in silence."* This is in keeping with other scriptures that teach us about the roles of husbands and wives in marriage.

Let's look at the other passage. Again, we see Paul's words: *"Let your women keep silence in the churches: for it is not permitted unto them to speak; but they are commanded to be under obedience as also saith the law. And if they will learn any thing let them ask their husbands at home: for it is a shame for women to speak in the church"* (1 Corinthians 14:34-35).

Clearly, this passage is talking to husbands and wives; not

men or women, in general. Again, this is consistent with God's plan for spiritual authority in the marriage relationship.

The consensus of these passages would indicate that women *may* teach or lead men, but they are *not* permitted to teach or usurp authority over their own husbands. What is the bottom line? All women are *not* to be submitted to all men. Women as a gender are *not* inferior or under the rule of men as a gender. A married woman should be submissive to her own husband in not "teaching or usurping his authority," but this does not apply to her relationship with other men.

Can you see that?

In marriage, God's highest and best is a love relationship where agreement and mutual submission to the Lord and one another is the way of life. God's plan is that husbands and wives live and work together as a team—not as competitors (Ephesians 5:21, Amos 3:3). The idea is that both the husband and wife defer and submit to one another in love, endeavoring to outdo one another when it comes to preferring one another. However, when there is disagreement or differing opinions, the husband is the God-appointed head and he ought to lead by loving his wife like Christ loves the church. Likewise, the wife ought to have a submissive spirit and behavior toward her husband like she does towards Jesus.

The Biblical idea is that a wife is not to "teach" or "lead" her husband in the sense of bossing him around or usurping his authority or rank. In modern language, a Jesus-loving, Spirit-filled wife ought to choose to be submitted (as in rank) to her own husband and not have a rebellious or manipulative spirit towards him by trying to pull rank and "teach him a thing or two!" In the same way, a Jesus-loving, Spirit-filled husband should love his wife and not operate like an ego-driven, pride-led dictator in commanding his wife's behavior. The New Living Translation describes this Spirit-filled marriage beautifully:

> *Instead, let the Holy Spirit fill and control you. Then you will sing psalms and hymns and spiritual songs among yourselves, making music to the Lord in your hearts. And you will always give thanks for everything to God the Father in the name of our Lord Jesus Christ. And further, you will submit to one another out of reverence for Christ. You wives will submit to your husbands as you do to the Lord. For a husband is the head of his wife as Christ is the head of his body, the church; he gave his life to be her Savior. As the church submits to Christ, so you wives must submit to your husbands in everything. And you husbands must love your wives with the same love Christ showed the church. He gave up his life for her to make her holy and clean, washed by baptism and God's word. He did this to present her to himself as a glorious church without a spot or wrinkle or any other blemish. Instead, she will be holy and without fault. In the same way, husbands ought to love their wives as they love their own bodies. For a man is actually loving himself when he loves his wife. No one hates his own body but lovingly cares for it, just as Christ cares for his body, which is the church. And we are his body. As the Scriptures say, 'A man leaves his father and mother and is joined to his wife, and the two are united into one.' This is a great mystery, but it is an illustration*

of the way Christ and the church are one. So again I say, each man must love his wife as he loves himself, and the wife must respect her husband, (Ephesians 5:18-33, NLT).

IS SUBMISSION A BAD WORD?

Since there is so much confusion and emotion on the subject of submission in marriage, let me share an email I received from a frustrated wife not long ago. Her email was in response to a newspaper column I had written, where I had mentioned the idea of wives submitting to their husbands.

Whoa. Pleeeeease. My marriage, like so many others I know, would disintegrate in a heartbeat if my husband and I took that attitude (the attitude of wives being submissive to their husbands). He'd be as uncomfortable with it as I would be. We're a team. We complement each other. Sometimes he's ying and I'm yang; sometimes it's the other way around.

We take note of what our family needs and use that to guide our decisions and actions as husband and wife—not blindly saying, 'Duh, you da man. Me just dumb woman. You decide!' Sometimes I need to be 'the decider,' and sometimes he does. We have different strengths and every marriage is different. Every single one.

In no way, I believe, does God expect that in each and every marriage the female is to take on a submissive role, by default. I've read the arguments from women who try to make it sound really 'okay' to be submissive: 'God tells husbands to love and cherish their wives, so it ends up being fair for both spouses in the end, blah blah. . .'"

A Wife and Mom Who Stands Right BESIDE (Not Behind) Her Husband

Here are excerpts of my response to this woman:

I agree with what you said. The team concept is actually more biblical than the suppressive idea of 'submission'—and no doubt, husbands and wives are supposed to operate as 'one'. I also agree with you that husbands and wives are supposed to compliment one another and work together and allow their strengths to fill in the other person's weaknesses. My husband and I operate as a team in life, family and ministry and yet—here's the big yet—God does tell women to be 'submissive to their own husbands.'

So, what is that all about? Be a doormat? Be a dumb, can't think, can't make a decision, 'you da man' type of woman? Absolutely not! The word 'submissive' is actually a military term and has to do with rank. The definition of submit/submissive/ subjection is primarily a military term: 'to rank under.'[2] The bottom line is simply this. In general, husbands and wives should be mutually submissive and loving towards one another.

However, in the event of a disagreement, or disunity where the wife wants to go 'north' and the husband wants to go 'south,' the biblical pattern is that both parties would first be willing to reason, listen to one another's views, walk in love, compromise, find unity and so on—and if there is still disagreement, then the husband has the highest rank and he gets to make the final call.

This is God's order and wives must respect and 'be submissive' to that decision. In a healthy marriage, this doesn't have to happen too often. Most wise men listen to their wives' input, and most wise women listen to their husbands' wisdom and they try to find a place of agreement and compromise. However, if and when push-comes-to-shove then the Lord says, 'wives be submissive to your husbands'... and 'husbands love your wives.'

It's pretty simple and common sense stuff, but people have tried to make the passages on submission say all sorts of negative things that are not within the context. I hope this makes sense.

This woman wrote back. She respectfully disagreed, but she appreciated hearing a Biblical view. She's not alone. In our culture, a lot of people have a convoluted view of the role of husbands and wives and the whole realm of submission.

JESUS BROKE THE RULES

In New Testament times, the cultural view of women and wives was suppressive. Women were not highly regarded and were often viewed as nothing more than property that should be dominated.

Nelson's Illustrated Bible Dictionary tells us that women were not esteemed in Jewish culture.

> *In order to understand the Old Testament view of woman, one must turn to the Book of Genesis. When God created mankind, He created both "male and female" (Genesis 1:27; 5:2). Both were created in God's image and both were given the responsibility of exercising authority over God's creation. The man was created before the woman. Because the man needed companionship and a helper, God caused the man to sleep. From him He created a woman, "a helper comparable to him" (Genesis 2:18, 20). Man is incomplete without woman. Because she is called a "helper" does not imply that she is inferior to man. The same Hebrew word translated as helper is used of God in His relationship to Israel (Psalms 33:20; 70:5). The culture that developed around the Israelites in ancient times did not always have this perspective of woman. Certain Old Testament passages tend to reflect an attitude that woman was little more than a thing and that a woman should be entirely subordinate to man. This tendency became pronounced before the coming of Christ. One of the Jewish prayers that dated from that era declared, "I thank Thee that I am not a woman." Jesus lived and taught a better way-the way of love.[3]*

In light of the mindset of the early church, it's easy to see why many women did not have a high profile—in life or marriage—let alone in the church. The two controversial passages about the role of women were written in the climate of a culture that did not value women.

Thankfully, Jesus valued women. Jesus broke those rules when He came on the scene. He called, validated, and commissioned women. Let's look at Jesus' view on women teachers, preachers, and leaders.

Before we move on to Chapter 5, let's look at several other dynamic and effective women leaders in the church: *Lisa Young, Sandy Scheer* and *Wendy Treat.*

WOMEN LEADERS IN THE CHURCH:
LISA YOUNG
SANDY SCHEER & WENDY TREAT

Lisa Young

Sandy Scheer

Wendy Treat

LISA YOUNG

Ed and Lisa Young pastor Fellowship Church, known as one of the most creative churches on earth. In addition to the main campus in Grapevine, Fellowship Church operates five more satellite campuses in the greater Dallas/Fort Worth area, two in Miami, Florida and a location in London, England.

God has used Ed and Lisa Young to impact my husband Jeff and me in more ways than we can count. The first time we met them was at their annual C3 Conference in 2003. We were blown away by everything we experienced, and it was at that conference that we felt God's "permission" to do church in some of the creative ways that had been bottled up in our hearts for years. Later, we had the privilege of being a "fly on the wall," along with 18 others pastors and wives, to shadow Ed and Lisa and their team for three days of behind-the-scenes meetings, sharing meals and asking questions through their Total Access experience to see how they did ministry up close and personally. To say that these things were a turning point in our lives and ministry is an understatement. The trajectory and growth of our church took a huge leap forward and it still continues to this day.

I was impressed then—as I have been on many occasions—in watching Lisa. She is a devoted wife and mother and communicates God's Word with warmth and grace, inspiring others to pursue a more intimate relationship with Him. Her passion is to see herself and others embrace the joys of walking with Christ in every day experiences. Each month, Lisa hosts Flavour, a ministry designed specifically for women at Fellowship Church. Flavour was born out of Lisa's desire to show women their true value and worth in God's eyes, as well as their potential to uniquely influence the world around them. In addition to joining Ed on stage for special messages, Lisa is a gifted writer and has enjoyed co-authoring several books. Time and again—through C3 Conferences, on a mission trip to Haiti with her and other pastors' wives/daughters, at other conferences and as she and Ed were guests at our church, I have seen her devotion, her grace, her wisdom and the anointing on her life impact those around her. Thousands of women look to Lisa as a role model and example of a woman in leadership in the church. Her walk with God and her experience in ministry in the local church is time-tested. I hope after you read her profile, you are inspired by her example!

In asking Lisa several questions, here's how she answered these important topics:

YOUR CALLING:

Q: How would you describe your call to ministry?

LY: I have two "calls" on my life to do ministry. I fell in love with Ed, my high school sweetheart, and knew that he had a touch from God on his life. My first call came through Ed. I knew that I was to be his wife and that whatever God wanted him to do, I would be there with him.

The second call came about ten years ago. After being in ministry for many years, I went through a time of "drought" and uncertainty in my role at Fellowship Church.

I believe this was truly a time of searching for me. I asked questions of other women in ministry, studied Scripture, and prayed for direction to see what God was leading me toward. It was at that time that I jumped into ministry full force, leading out with creative development, teaching the women in Flavour, speaking anytime there was a need or an opportunity. Our motto at Fellowship Church is that we, as a team, are willing to do "anything, everything, or nothing," and it was at this time that I truly began to live that motto out!

Q: Are you called to a leading and/or teaching role in the local church and if so, in what roles have you functioned?

LY: Yes, I have been called to lead out in key leadership and teaching in our church. We have a mantra at Fellowship Church that our staff and volunteers understand: anything, everything, or nothing. We don't typically tag people with titles, because we really do have that mindset of "Whatever it takes." I've worked in nearly every area of our church's ministry – from the preschool to helping with weekend experiences. My role has changed over the 24 years of Fellowship Church. Sometimes it's been more behind-the-scenes, while other times it has been up front. But I've tried to fulfill any role that God has given to me to fulfill, and to be the kind of influence and leader that has helped to grow His kingdom.

Q: Who, what and when do you lead and/or teach in your church?

LY: I have been leading our women's ministry, called Flavour Sisterhood, for the past several years. I'm also a part of our church's leadership team, which is responsible for maintaining the vision and direction of the church. I play a role in any major decision for the church. For the past 24 years, I've been on "staff" at the church, even before I was technically on staff. As a pastor's wife, there's never a time that I'm not leading in some fashion.

Our Flavour Sisterhood (women's ministry) meets every Wednesday night. I lead out in this, though we occasionally have other speakers/teachers. I also will occasionally teach during the main weekend experiences, depending on the topic of the sermon or series. Ed and I will also co-preach/ teach when it is appropriate. I believe it is important for women to have a role in teaching in every area of the church.

Q: Have you embraced and enjoyed your calling and role over the years?

LY: There was a time several years ago when I balked at leading out. I thought my role was to be Ed's wife and to support him. Through much prayer and some great friends who lead out in other ministries, I came to understand that God has placed me in my position to have a leadership role. Through that season, God birthed in me the vision for Flavour. Now, I have an opportunity to travel some and speak, as well as to lead the women of Fellowship Church, and I love it!

Q: Have you ever been reluctant to embrace your call to leadership or teaching in the church?

LY: I was reluctant for a while to take a key lead role. I was comfortable being Ed's wife, supporting him and helping the vision of the church from behind-the-scenes. However, God woke me up to my calling and I realized that He has placed me where I am because He wants me to play a key role.

My reluctance was never a result of a lack of opportunity or any kind of negativity towards women leading out. Our church has always been very open and receptive to women in leadership roles. If someone had a problem with my role, they most likely left Fellowship Church!

Q: Have you ever thought God made a mistake when He called you to leadership and teaching, because you are a woman?

LY: No. I have looked back now and realized that it was me who was making a mistake by not following God's call on my life to lead out. This was due mostly to personal insecurity and the exposure early in my life to male-only teachers. Thankfully, God has allowed me to have the role I have and to be the kind of influence I can be to the women (and to the men) of Fellowship Church.

Q: As a woman in ministry in the local church, what has been the biggest challenge for you to overcome?

LY: My biggest challenge is not comparing myself to other speakers and leaders. Another big one for me is being disciplined in study and preparation for speaking.

Q: What are your thoughts about churches that do not ordain, license or allow women in leadership ministry roles?

LY: I think there's something missing when women aren't allowed to lead out in any capacity in the church. I believe God has equipped women with a heart, a vision, and a passion for His church that can be significant when it comes to accomplishing the mission of the church.

Q: What experiences and/or responses have you had when you are told that it is not Biblical for women to be in ministry or that pastoral ministry is only for males? Or, what would you say to a woman who has been told she cannot minister until her children are grown?

LY: I examine the whole counsel and context of Scripture rather than listening to the criticism or any voice that has that tone. Human voices mean nothing in light of God's supernatural touch and call!

I would say that you absolutely can minister, no matter how old your children are! Granted, when your children are little, the scheduling is much more difficult. However, there are opportunities in every season of life to be an influence to those around you. You can always have a voice in the lives of others around you to point them to Jesus Christ. That's what ministering is all about. And God places you right where you are, as the book of Esther says, "For such a time as this."

Q: Do you think people expect a woman to be more qualified than a man to take on a ministry role?

LY: We have some very strong, very qualified women who lead out at Fellowship Church. But a degree doesn't qualify anyone, man or woman, to take a ministry role. It's about the heart and passion for the church and for our Savior. What people expect and what God expects are often not the same thing. If God calls, then they are qualified – whether they are a man or a woman! We benchmark all teaching on God's Word, not opinion. If a person can teach God's Word effectively and accurately, that's what truly counts.

YOUR HUSBAND:

Q: Do you work as a team with your husband in ministry?

LY: Yes. Ed and I work together constantly in the ministry. We co-teach, co-write, and co-lead in several areas. I'm there with him for key staff meetings and am part of the leadership team at our church, alongside my husband.

Q: Describe his role in supporting or encouraging you in your calling.

LY: Ed is the most encouraging person I know. He has always been that way, challenging me to step up in areas, encouraging me to take risks. He's my biggest supporter when it comes to anything in life. My leadership in the church is just another area of that support. Ed and I make a great team. We understand each other's roles and never do anything that would be threatening to the leadership or influence of the other. Each of us has unique gifts separately, and together we are better!

Q: If you could coach a young husband/pastor in how to encourage/release his wife and her gifts in the church, what would you say to him?

LY: I would remind him that God has called him to love his wife unconditionally. That love plays out in every area of their relationship. I would encourage him to remember the gift that she is to him, and that God has provided him with her as a helper. In fact, Eve was the complimentary helper to Adam back in the Garden, and I believe that marriages today are more successful when the partners support and encourage one another. I would also remind him that his young bride has gifts that he doesn't have (just as he has gifts that she doesn't have), and the church will only be strengthened when those gifts are used!

YOUR FAMILY:

Q: Are your kids involved with you in ministry? Do you have daughters who feel called to leadership or a teaching role in the ministry?

LY: Yes. Our children (all four) absolutely love the church! Currently, two of our four children are on staff here at Fellowship Church. Our son EJ is in the design department and is using his creative gifts to help with photography, graphics, video, etc. Our daughter LeeBeth plays a lead role on our production team, as well as overseeing EdYoung.com. Our daughter Laurie is very involved in the church in her college town. I believe she has a call on her life to ministry. I have absolute hope that our children will continue to embrace their calling. Ed and I have never forced them to go into the ministry. And because of that, their call has been one that God has placed on their lives. They have embraced that, have fallen in love with the church, and are excited to be part of what God is doing through the local church!

YOUR ROLE:

Q: Have you felt celebrated and recognized and allowed to fully use your gifts and calling?

LY: I feel encouraged, celebrated, and appreciated every day. It starts with Ed. Like I said, he is the biggest supporter I have. After that, the staff and volunteers are a huge source of encouragement for me. I'm thankful to have that network of support as I seek to fulfill God's call in my life. I also have received very positive feedback from the men and women of Fellowship Church. They tell me my perspective is vital in their spiritual growth as well.

Q: If you were honest, what percentage would you say you feel in terms of being fulfilled and satisfied that you are fulfilling your calling and purpose as a woman in the church?

LY: 90% fulfilled. That's not a stretch. When you embrace God's call on your life, when you take risks to fulfill that call, and when you get the opportunity to be part of what He is doing through the local church, there's nothing more satisfying in the world. I always pray that my "humanness" will not allow me to hold anything back from God.

To connect with Lisa Young, find her at:

www.FellowshipChurch.com

www.FlavourSisterhood.com

Twitter: @LisaYoungFC

Instagram: @LisaYoungFC

SANDY SCHEER

We love Pastors Bill and Sandy Scheer. The Scheers pastor Guts Church in Tulsa, Oklahoma and that tells you everything you need to know! They have guts! They take the church, the gospel and reaching people seriously. They push the limits to preach the gospel. Their church tag line defines their mission well: *Help People Win.* While they are passionate about the gospel, they are as normal and down-to-earth as any couple you'll ever meet.

Over the past several years, I have come to appreciate Bill and Sandy's heart for people, their no-nonsense approach to ministry and the way they and their family interact and do ministry together. I especially admire the innovative approach Sandy takes to minister to the women at Guts, aka *The Guts Girls.*

Perhaps, one of the best things about Bill and Sandy is their willingness to share their experiences, ideas and successes with other churches, including ours. Whether it's the success of *The Nightmare* (their October outreach) the *Tougher Than Hell Motorcycle Rally, Guts Girls Give Back* or their *Friday Groceries* and *Distribution Center* outreach—they are a great example of what it looks like to do church with guts!

What I especially love about Sandy is that every time we get the chance to connect—whether we're sitting in a Starbucks catching up or in a beach chair somewhere talking about God, church or family—I always laugh and am inspired by her. I often wish we had more time to hang out, and I know you will feel the same way as you read her profile.

YOUR CALL:

Q: Describe your call to ministry. How old were you, what did you envision you would be doing, what Scriptures did God give you or what experience did you have that made you feel you were called by Him?

SS: I attended Ole Miss as a freshman and during that year God spoke to me to go to ORU. I received my Bachelors Degree in Counseling. I got married in 1984 and we started Guts Church in 1990. The 34th chapter of Ezekiel was the Scripture the Lord gave Bill and I to start our church in Tulsa, Oklahoma.

Q: Are you called to a leading and/or teaching role in the local church, if so, who, what and when do you lead in your church?

SS: I am called to pastor with my husband. My emphasis is on women of all ages in our church. I've ministered to every age group.

Q: Describe the joy, fruit and satisfaction you've experienced:

SS: It has been rewarding to see people that have never had a relationship with the Lord have their lives completely changed by the Word of God.

Q: Have you been reluctant to embrace your call to leadership or teaching in the church? If so, in what ways?

SS: Yes, but not because I am a woman. It was because of

fear, due to a previous experience, that the enemy tried to use against me. It was something that I had to overcome and completely do afraid!

Q: Knowing what you know now about life, ministry and church, what would you tell yourself if you could rewind the clock and go back 15-20 years?

SS: Do it afraid and trust that God will be with your mouth and teach you what to say!

YOUR CHALLENGES:

Q: What has been the biggest challenge for you to overcome as a woman in ministry?

SS: Finding a balance between raising my children and leading in ministry. My family always comes first.

Q: What would you say to a woman who has been told she cannot speak, teach or lead in the church because she is a woman, or she can only teach women or she has to wait until her children are grown?

SS: I would say you need to get in the Word and find out what it says about this. The women need to hear from you.

YOUR HUSBAND:

Q: Describe your husband's role in supporting or encouraging you in your calling?

SS: He has always been very supportive. For 22 years he has been very persistent in encouraging me to lead the women in our church. I feel very fulfilled in working with my husband. We are a team. We have a healthy family and a healthy church. I feel they go hand in hand.

Q: If you could coach a young husband/pastor on how to encourage/release his wife and her gifts in the church, what would you say to him?

SS: Her voice is just as crucial to the health of your church as it is to the health of your children. She needs to be in front of the church. They need to see how you interact and how you both live your lives.

YOUR FAMILY:

Q: Are other members of your family involved with you in ministry? If so, who and what roles?

SS: All three of our children are involved in our ministry. Taylor is involved in our Innovation department, Brooklyn works at the church for Guts Girls and our outreaches, and Kennedy is involved in our student ministries. Over the past 22 years, we have worked as a family in all areas of ministry. Our children are our greatest asset because they understand us as parents and ministers. They get it!

Q: Do you have daughters who feel called to leadership or a teaching role in the ministry? What hopes do you have for your daughters?

SS: Both of our daughters feel called to leadership and teaching in the ministry. They both have spoken publicly at our church. We've raised them to genuinely love the church. My hope is for them to fulfill the call of God on their lives.

MENTORING:

Q: What would you say to young girls these days about being in the ministry—particularly women called to leadership in the church?

SS: You've got to know you're called. If you are, it'll be the best decision you'll ever make!

Q: What else do we need to know about you and your calling to leadership and/or teaching in the church?

SS: I am entering into the empty nest season. It's very fulfilling but I feel a transition that my role will take a little bit of a different turn as I will have more time to devote to things that I was unable to do while caring for my children.

You can connect with Sandy at:

www.gutschurch.com

Twitter: gutsgirl1

Instagram: @sandyscheer

Email: pastorsandy@gutschurch.com

WENDY TREAT

Wendy Treat is a new friend for me. For years, I knew of she and her husband Casey Treat and the influence they were having in the Northwest. When I recently met Wendy at a Women's Conference, I instantly knew I liked her. She's funny, honest, bold and full of the Word. Her bio describes a church leader who's making a difference.

She is a wife, mother, grandmother, pastor, teacher, international conference speaker, and role model. She writes and teaches from a practical standpoint, seasoning it with her unique sense of humor. With a desire to make a difference in the lives of people, Wendy enrolled in Seattle Bible College where she met and later married her husband, Casey Treat. In 1980, they founded Christian Faith Center with just 30 people. After more than three decades, the church ministers to many thousands of people in three locations around the Seattle, Washington, area.

The Treat's host a weekly television program called, *Your Unlimited Life*, which is broadcast nationally and internationally. Wendy also makes frequent guest appearances on other programs, including an interview on Fox News' O'Reilly Factor. She is featured in blogs, newspapers, and magazines. Wendy loves to read, travel, entertain, and along with her husband is an avid bicyclist.

I know you will be encouraged by the wisdom of her experience as a woman leader in the church.

YOUR CALL:

Q: How would you describe your call to ministry and your role in your church?

WT: I'm a pastor. I always knew I had a passion for God's House and God's people. My call to ministry is a call to serve people and help them see the fullness of living for Jesus. To me, it is the greatest calling in the world.

I have been called "the little boss" as long as I can remember. I was very grateful the bossy Wendy was trained to be a leader in the Kingdom. I began teaching shortly after I was saved at age 17. I've never stopped teaching the Bible. I teach a weekly Bible study, Ladies in Leadership Webinar, regular worship services, plus travel to teach at women's conferences, church services, and events around the world. God has blessed me with this gift and what an honor it is!

Q: Have you ever thought God made a mistake when He called you to leadership and teaching?

WT: Did I ever feel God made a mistake? Yup! I have truly had to work through my own sense of inadequacy! My thoughts have ranged from: not funny enough, spiritual enough, smart enough, plain and simple, not "enough" in every area. I am so grateful God placed so many people around me who helped me see through God's eyes, rather than my inadequate earth eyesight.

YOUR CHALLENGES:

Q: What has been the biggest challenge for you to overcome as a woman in ministry?

WT: My biggest challenges have come from my own small way of thinking. Not seeing what God sees in me and in those around me has crippled me at times. My success and failure starts with myself and I know that I have been my own biggest enemy at times, and I am thankful God never gives up on us!

Q: What would you say to a woman who has been told she cannot speak, teach or lead in the church because she is a woman, or she can only teach women, or she has to wait until her children are grown?

WT: Women have asked me all my Christian life what to do with those who do not believe in women. I always use my great-grandmother, grandmother and mother as my example. Each one of them was married to a pastor (not considered pastors themselves). Each of them, all their lives, served alongside them committed to giving, loving and doing whatever they could to build the Kingdom. I'm thankful they did not stop serving because they weren't honored properly or given a title. I am committed to do what God has called me to do and serve any way that I can. I cannot and will not be stopped from my God-given calling due to other people's problems. Women around the world are called to do great things, and I pray and believe they will read these words and the words of this book and believe that they can do all God has called them to do.

YOUR HUSBAND:

Q: How would you describe your husband's role in supporting or encouraging you in your calling?

WT: I have been extremely blessed with my husband, Casey, who has always believed in me and encouraged me to pursue my visions and dreams. When we started our ministry, we did everything together and have maintained that unity over the last 40 years. There is nothing we can't do if God called us to do it. Personally, I have seen a different degree of resistance to my leadership and other women leaders, but I am diligent and tenacious and I won't give up until the job is done!

Casey has always been my biggest supporter and encouragement. He saw God's call upon my life and believed that I could—and would—achieve great things for God's Kingdom. With his quiet and confident way, he promoted me as a teacher in our main services, endorsed me in business settings, and nudged me in the back when I wanted to sink my heels in to the ground. He protected me from other's complaints and truly believed our teamwork was one of the greatest weapons in our arsenal to win the Northwest for Jesus.

Q: Do you ever have conflict about your role or struggle with not wanting him to feel threatened or in competition with you?

WT: Two strong people will always have to keep conversation going on, submitting to the roles and calls we have. I also have always recognized Casey as the senior pastor, which means he's boss and his word is the final word. When you lift others up, you are lifted.

Q: If you could coach a young husband/pastor in how to encourage/release his wife and her gifts in the church, what would you say to him?

WT: I would encourage him to allow her to dream big and pursue those dreams. The couple should get in agreement on what the dream looks like and then it's time to have bulldog tenacity and pursue it.

Q: Are other members of your family involved with you in ministry? What hopes do you have for your daughter (and other young ladies) who feel called to ministry?

WT: Yes. Caleb is our eldest son (age 29) and he is a pastor and executive leader of our church. Tasha is our only daughter (age 27) and she is also a pastor and leader at CFC. This is a whole other book, but I would say it is vitally important to honor and respect each other in what God has called and equipped you to do. We keep it a central priority to always respect each other and work together to build God's House. I love watching the beauty of generations building on the last. So I love watching, leading and helping any way I can. I had a legacy of women behind me who were leaders in church and I am proud to be able to pass that legacy on to my daughter and the other girls in ministry. God is raising up remarkable young women!

YOU:

Q: Have you ever felt like a misfit in ministry and church life?

WT: Misfit – yes! As I've grown and look back at my life, it is easy to see the times where I felt like I was hitting my head against a wall, not reaching the goals I wanted to reach. I could not figure out why I felt the way I felt or did not always fit in. Growing in Jesus and becoming more secure in Him has helped me live bigger from the inside out, and has enabled me to stay strong and not get discouraged during the tough times.

Q: Knowing what you know now about life, ministry and church, what would you tell yourself if you could rewind the clock and go back 15-20 years?

WT: Be happier. Laugh more. People come and go—be ok with it.

You can connect with Wendy at:

Website: www.wendytreat.com

Email: wendyt@christianfaithcenter.org

Instagram: @wendytreat

Twitter: @wendytreat

Facebook Fan Page: Wendy Treat

CHAPTER 5

WHAT DOES JESUS THINK ABOUT WOMEN LEADERS AND PREACHERS?

So, what does Jesus really think about women? Women in ministry? Women preachers? Women leaders?

If anyone could have set the record straight, it would have been Jesus. Right? If anyone could have made the case that women should be silent, it would have been Jesus. If anyone could have shown us that all women were to be subservient to all men, it would have been Jesus.

Interestingly, Jesus didn't seem to have a problem with women leaders and preachers. In fact, He called women to preach and on a few occasions, He told the women to preach to men!

Let's look at two women Jesus called to preach.

JESUS TOLD MARY TO PREACH

After His resurrection, Jesus told Mary to preach the Gospel to men! "... **go to my brethren and say unto them**, *I ascend unto my Father, and your Father; and to my God and your God*," (John 20:17, emphasis mine). Did Jesus violate His own command that women must be silent and not teach men? The first preacher God called after the resurrection was a woman, and Jesus told her to preach to men!

Jesus put all His initial "eggs" for the furtherance of the gospel and the launch of His Church in the heart and mouth of a woman. What if she had been taught that a woman should be silent—not leading, teaching or preaching, and especially that she should never teach a man?

Think about it. Jesus called Mary to be the first leader and preacher of His resurrection. If women were not supposed to have any leadership role, Jesus blew it! Why didn't Jesus make it absolutely clear and without question that women were not to have any leadership, preaching or speaking role in the ministry? Why didn't He make it crystal clear that women should be silent and never teach men? This would have been the perfect opportunity! If that was His will, He never would have called Mary to be the first one to witness His resurrection, the first one to preach the good news to men. Thankfully, Jesus didn't validate the incorrect way of thinking, He definitively said women can lead and teach and preach by calling Mary to be the first leader, preacher and teacher of His resurrection—the foundation upon which the church is built! In fact, Jesus put an exclamation point on it when He said, "*...go to my brethren and say.*" In modern lingo, He was saying, *"Mary, go preach to the men!"* What would have happened if Peter and John had said, *"Stop it Mary! You are not allowed to teach men. Be silent!"* Why would Jesus put such a responsibility upon a woman if He did not validate women as preachers or leaders?

Matthew Henry's commentary makes an interesting point about Mary's calling to preach the message of the resurrection, *"This was her reward for her constancy in adhering to Christ, and enquiring after him; and a tacit rebuke to the apostles, who had not been so close as she was in attending on the dying Jesus, nor so early as she was in meeting the rising Jesus; she becomes an apostle to the apostles."*[1]

JESUS AND THE WOMAN AT THE WELL

What do we do with Jesus and the woman at the well? After she met Jesus, she preached to all the men in her city!

And at this point His disciples came, and they marveled that He talked with a woman; yet no one said, "What do You seek?" or, "Why are You talking with her?" **The woman then left her waterpot, went her way into the city, and said to the men**, *"Come, see a Man who told me all things that I ever did. Could this be the Christ?" Then they went out of the city and came to Him. . .* **And many of the Samaritans of that city believed in Him because of the word of the woman** *who testified, "He told me all that I ever did." So when the Samaritans had come to Him,* they urged Him to stay with them; and He stayed there two days. And many more believed because of His own word. Then they said to the woman, "Now we believe, not because of what you said, for we ourselves have heard Him and we know that this is indeed the Christ, the Savior of the world" (John 4:27-30, 39-42, NKJV, emphasis mine). When this woman opened her mouth, the entire city got saved!

Talk about a lady preacher!

Notice, the disciples were surprised that Jesus was talking with a woman. That's because the culture they knew didn't esteem women. They only knew the culture they had grown up in—a culture that didn't regard women—and they were shocked to see Jesus breaking the rules by talking to a woman.

Jesus broke the cultural rules. He set this woman free and she was compelled to preach to the men in her city. What if she had been taught that women must be silent and they cannot teach men? Would an entire city have been left unsaved? It doesn't appear that Jesus rebuked her at any time for her boldness to preach and teach men about Him. In fact, perhaps Jesus applauded her boldness as she fulfilled His prophetic statements that those who were filled with the Spirit would be His witnesses in Samaria and the uttermost parts of the earth (Acts 1:8). Thankfully, these Samaritan men were humble and hungry enough to listen and learn.

Fortunately, Jesus broke the rules and validated women during His earthly ministry. Today, He's still calling women to preach, teach, lead, testify and serve in "apostolic" roles—where both men and women are impacted.

JESUS AND NEW TESTAMENT WOMEN

The day of Pentecost was a turning point in human history! Jesus sent the Holy Spirit to be poured out on all flesh and one wonderful benefit was that He set godly "handmaidens" free to preach and continue in the liberty He had given to them in His earthly ministry.

Again, we are reminded of the words of Joel 2:28 as they are repeated in Acts 2:18, *"And it shall come to pass in the last days, saith God, I will pour out my Spirit upon all flesh: and **your sons and your daughters shall prophesy**, and your young men shall see visions, and your old men shall dream dreams: And **on my servants and on my handmaidens I will pour out in those days of my Spirit; and they shall prophesy**"* (Acts 2:17-18, emphasis mine).

The International Standard Bible Encyclopedia gives us a great summary of the freedom Jesus brought to women.

> *A new era dawned for woman with the advent of Christianity . . . From the first, women held official positions of influence in the church. Phoebe (Rom 16:1) was evidently a deaconess, whom Paul terms "a servant of the church," "a helper of many" and of himself also. Those women who "labored with me in the gospel" (Phil 4:3) undoubtedly participated with him in preaching . . . Her culture, grace,*

scholarship, ability, religious devotion and spiritual enduement make it evident that she is often as truly called of God to public address and instruction as man. It is evident in the New Testament and in the writings of the Apostolic Fathers that women, through the agency of two ecclesiastical orders, were assigned official duties in the conduct and ministrations of the early church . . . The social and legal status of woman instantly improved when Christianity gained recognition in the Empire. Her property rights as wife were established by law, and her husband made subject to accusation for marital infidelity. Her inferiority, subjection and servitude among all non-Jewish and non-Christian races, ancient and modern, are the severest possible arraignment of man's intelligence and virtue . . . The freedom wherewith Christ did set us free includes her complete liberation to equality of opportunity with man. In mental endowment, in practical ability, in all the higher ministries of life and even in statecraft, she has proved herself the equal of man. Christianity always tends to place woman side by side with man in all the great achievements of education, art, literature, the humanities, social service and missions. The entire movement of modern society toward her perfect enfranchisement is the distinct and inevitable product of the teaching of Jesus.2

Let's look at another important consideration regarding women in the church.

CHAPTER 6

IS GOD A GOOD MANAGER OF HIS RESOURCES?

For a moment, let's look at this subject logically. I'm confident that Jesus is absolutely the smartest, wisest CEO ever! If He wants the gospel preached to the ends of the earth, is He going to set aside 50% of His potential workforce? Is that what any wise human resources director would do?

I know God doesn't always go with large numbers, ratios, and human logic; so, don't get tripped up by the comparison. The Lord has been known to use small numbers of faith-filled people to accomplish big feats. Case in point: Gideon! At the same time, the Lord is not a waster. Let's give this some consideration.

IS JESUS A GOOD CEO?

Jesus is the Head of the Church. He's the Lord of the Harvest. Certainly, He knows how to run His operation and build His church. Jesus said the harvest was plentiful, but the workers were few.

"When he saw the crowds, he had compassion on them, because they were harassed and helpless, like sheep without a shepherd. Then he said to his disciples, 'The harvest is plentiful but the workers are few. Ask the Lord of the harvest, therefore, to send out workers into his harvest field'" (Matthew 9:36-38, NIV).

With that reality in mind, He sent out His "recruiting call" to "whoever has ears to hear" in His last recorded words, known as the Great Commission.

Think about it...

In the Great Commission, Jesus said, *"All authority has been given to Me in heaven and on earth. Go therefore and make disciples of all the nations, baptizing them in the name of the Father and of the Son and of the Holy Spirit, teaching them to observe all things that I have commanded you; and lo, I am with you always, even to the end of the age. Amen"* (Matthew 28:18-20, NKJV).

The call went out! Jesus commanded us to preach the gospel. Who was Jesus talking to? Just the 12 disciples? Just men? Did Jesus exclude women? No. The Great Commission is for men and women.

The Great Commission includes preaching the gospel and teaching the Word to make disciples of all nations. Men and women are called to preach the gospel and teach the Word to make disciples. This may be done through any number of vehicles: one-on-one evangelism and discipleship, massive crusades and follow-up, small groups, missions work, Sunday school, Vacation Bible Schools, concerts, seminaries and Bible schools, local churches and worldwide church plants.

The harvest is plentiful, but the laborers are few. Jesus, the Lord of the harvest, told us to pray for more laborers—which must include both men and women for this mighty task.

VALLEY FAMILY CHURCH

Let me share more of our story and the way God has led us to lead at Valley Family Church. I believe our journey will help you to navigate your own.

My husband and I have always believed that the local church is the most effective "combine harvester" and "disciple-making-leadership-development-operation" in any city. Reaching the harvest of lost, unchurched people and growing them into genuine followers of Christ can be accelerated through the ministry of a strong local church.

As we have led our church to fulfill our God-given mission of helping people "get it"—we each fulfill our respective roles in leading and teaching. First, we endeavor to do church in such a way as to help lost, unchurched people to come to know Jesus—to "get saved." Then, we teach the Word to those who are saved so they "get victory" in their own lives. Then, we are intentional about helping the victorious "get trained" to do the work of the ministry and finally, we do our best to motivate the trained to "get going" into their sphere of influence to reach more lost people. Everything we do is to this end.

We have often been asked how we do this as a husband-wife team. In other words, people want to know who does what? What are our specific roles? What does our organizational chart look like? How do we complement and not compete with one another? What roles do other men and women in our church hold? Perhaps our experience will spark ideas that will help you. Here's how we operate.

My husband and I are first-generation Christians and first-generation ministers in our respective families—meaning, we had to figure it out! We didn't have parents, grandparents or anyone else in our families who were born-again Christians or pastors to call upon or look to for wisdom, experience or help when it came to being followers of Christ, church planters or pastors. For us—that was perfect! At our core, we are independent pioneers, innovators and pastors, so God knew what He was doing when He called us!

In the mid-80's, God gave us a vision to plant a church somewhere in America. We knew we were to pioneer a church that would help people who didn't know what they didn't know, *get it*—help them get Jesus, get saved, get the basics, get filled, get healed, get victory, get trained and get going into all the world to help others *get it*!

We founded Valley Family Church in Kalamazoo, Michigan, in September 1991 with five adults and four kids. I was pregnant and Diane, (another lady in our core group) was pregnant so we knew that within nine months we would be growing by a minimum of two! Since that time, we have grown and watched the Lord touch thousands of lives with the life-changing power of the gospel!

BACK IN THE DAY

Since the day of our Grand Opening service in 1991, Jeff and I have worked together as a husband/wife, teaching and leadership team—much like Aquilla and Priscilla of Acts 18. Keep in mind in the early 90's, we did not personally know any other husband/wife pastoral teams where both the husband and the wife had a high leadership and platform profile, nor did we know one other woman who went by the title "pastor." In fact, it took us many years to apply that title to my role and to the other women on our staff who served in pastoral roles.

This was during the era when every church sign in town had the name of the church on top and right below it was: Pastor Big Shot's Name. Although we were a team, our Grand Opening sign fit right in with the culture of the day—it had the name of the church on top and right below it was: Pastor Jeff Jones—in a font size larger than the name of the church! (And, I'm the one who designed that sign!) We laugh about it now. Even though we were a husband/wife team in every way, on our church sign we gave the impression that my role was on the down-low—which it totally wasn't.

Most of the pastors' wives we knew in the 80's and 90's were stay-at-home moms or working behind the scenes, functioning as secretaries, singers and piano players; or they were responsible for the hospitality, women's ministry, or teaching ladies Bible studies. I admired and respected these pastors' wives, but I often felt like a fish-out-of-water, because, while all of these roles are valid, worthy and important in the church, this wasn't how God had wired me or my husband to operate.

We knew a few pastors' wives that, if the truth was known, were the "brains" of the operation. Yet they worked quietly, enabling their husbands to shine as the pastor. They did not desire any pulpit role, nor did they feel called to any public leadership role although, they were clearly involved in the leadership, vision, and direction of the church. (There may have been other husband/wife teams who shared the leadership, pulpit or pastoral title equally, we just didn't know about them. Thankfully, today, there are many more wonderful pastoral teams where both husband and wife teach and lead together in their respective roles.)

We longed for husband/wife pastoral team mentors, only to discover that God would lead us to blaze a trail over the next few decades. By God's grace, we've endeavored to follow the leading of the Spirit as we pioneered our own model of a husband/wife pastoral ministry team.

WORKING TOGETHER

One of the big secrets to our success is the word: *we*. My husband and I have been very intentional about saying "we" and not "I" when we talk about our roles in the church from the platform, in staff meetings and in conversation. Pioneering and pastoring a church has never felt like something "he" is doing, but rather, something "we" are doing together. We are very "together" focused.

The other big secret to our success—and specifically to my success as a leader in our church—is my husband. To his credit, he is a very humble and secure leader (most of the time!) with a huge heart, and he has been the one championing my role in our church. He's taken Proverbs 18:22 seriously, *"He who finds a wife finds a good thing, and obtains favor from the LORD" (NKJV).* I think he intentionally looked for the "good" in me and made a way for me to operate in the gifts and calling God had on my life. As a result, God's favor flows in his life.

In the early years of our ministry, while Jeff was doing most of the pastoral counseling, weddings, funerals and hospital visits, I was busy raising preschoolers during the day and working late into the night designing the church infrastructure, creative outreach, and discipleship systems for growth. On the weekends, Jeff preached the sermons and I taught our "Get a Grip on the Basics" classes. As the kids got older and were involved in school, sports and youth group, and as the demands of a growing church increased, we made tweaks to our schedules and adjusted our roles to find the best way to operate as a husband/wife team.

Working together in ministry has been a process of learning, making mistakes and figuring out our respective lanes. We both had to be flexible and okay with doing non-stereotypical things at home and at church. It took time to figure out who was good and gifted at what.

For example, at home, Jeff opened "Big Daddy's Bistro" where each morning he made breakfast and had devotions with the kids before they went off to school. He was also the Chief of Laundry—no small task for a family of six. My role at home was Chief Communicator, making sure our kids were emotionally connected and that the lines of communication were always open. It was also my job to keep our home clean, organized and decorated, and to believe God for annual family vacations.

When it came to the church, we worked together on most things. Of course, our first priority was to focus on our own personal relationship with the Lord. We both knew we had a responsibility to pray, to spend time in the Word, to stay full of faith and to be led by the Spirit.

On the practical side, we are both very entrepreneurial, so we planned, strategized, cast vision and led together. From 1991 until 2003, Jeff did most of the weekend preaching, but he had me speak on the weekends annually during the month of February and on Mother's Day. In 2003, he felt strongly that I was to do more speaking, so he decided to have us share the weekend preaching schedule 50/50 and we've been doing that ever since.

When it comes to speaking, we usually preach in a series format, so generally Jeff will preach every weekend for one month and then I will do the same for the following month. Several times a year, we do a marriage, parenting or vision-casting series together. Thankfully, we've gotten past the naysayers and our church family loves to hear from both of us. These days, we are enjoying a great deal of favor as a husband/wife team in our community.

On the back end, when it comes to leading our church during the "office hours", we have tried to identify our strengths and operate in such a way that each of our gifts are maximized.

Jeff is a pragmatic leader. He is a great Bible teacher and quite funny. He's also good with managing and stewarding the finances. He enjoys and is recharged through solitude, yet he is the most servant-hearted person I know. He has a real pastor's heart and enjoys helping people. He looks for ways to serve them in their highs (births, weddings and celebrations) and lows (family crisis', personal challenges and in times of need). He likes things to be orderly and structured. When he is in those pockets, he's happy and fruitful.

For me, I am an intuitive leader. I love teaching people the basics of God's Word in fun ways and seeing the lightbulbs turn on. I'm a people person and I get a great deal of joy in being with people and planning events. I am a visionary, big-picture thinker, so it's easy for me to see things and execute them strategically and systematically. I have discovered that I can get bored easily, so I thrive when I have freedom to pioneer, lead, launch, write and speak in innovative ways. When I am running in those lanes, I am happy and fulfilled.

Through understanding how we are uniquely wired, we have intentionally positioned ourselves to compliment one another, rather than frustrate or compete with each other. We have not done it perfectly. We've had a few interesting challenges along the way, like the hundred times someone in our church has walked up to Jeff and called him, "Pastor Beth" (I am not exaggerating!) or when a sweet woman I was shaking hands with after a service told me what a great job Jeff did—on the message I just preached! We've learned to smile and roll with it.

It has taken time to figure out how to work together as a husband and wife team. We have been velcroed to each other 24/7 for the past few decades and that comes with great joys as well as its own set of difficulties. Miscommunication, misunderstandings and hurt feelings are a part of the learning curve, but thankfully, we were both committed to the Lord, each other and communicating until we got to the end of each "tunnel of chaos!" Over time, we figured out how to maximize the grace God has put on our lives individually—and as a couple—and our children and church family have reaped the benefits of this approach to ministry.

In 2009 and 2010, Valley Family Church experienced phenomenal growth as God graced our church and Outreach Magazine named us one of the Top 100 Fastest Growing Churches in America. It was an exciting season of growth as we, our staff, and volunteers ran to keep up with what God was doing in our church! When we found out we made the 2009 list, my husband realized the editors were planning to only list his name as senior pastor below our church name in the magazine. So, he contacted the magazine and told them that they needed to include my name next to his. Apparently, they had never included a woman on the list previously. Jeff was very gracious and told them if they did not feel comfortable listing Jeff and Beth Jones together as the senior pastors, they could take our church off the list.

At that time, I told my husband it was no big deal and I was fine with not being mentioned. He said, "No, you are leading this church with me and your name is going to be mentioned or I don't want our church on the list." Well, it turns out—they added my name and I am the only woman listed in the top 100 fastest growing churches for those years. You can imagine, Jeff is my hero! I wish the same for every other woman who is working side-by-side with her husband.

THE PARALLELS IN CORPORATE LIFE, MARRIAGE AND FAMILY

As for our church organizational flow chart, our official titles are: Senior Pastors, Jeff and Beth Jones. Together, we lead the church, but if push-comes-to-shove, Jeff is the ultimate leader and the buck stops at *his* desk. We each have "official" job descriptions that define our specific roles and hold us accountable for using our unique gifts to lead our church.

In the day-to-day operations of leading our staff and ministry, perhaps we've functioned more like church entrepreneurs. We flow together in thinking organizationally and systematically about the three "P's" of a successful enterprise—things business-minded people think about: people, products, processes.

People: The kids, students and adults inside the church and the community outside the church walls.

Product: The life-changing power of the gospel and Word of God!

Processes: Our weekend services, prayer, outreaches and various spiritual growth tracks we employ.

In leading our staff and church family, we've operated like a family where he's the "Dad" of the house and I am the "Mom." This has created a healthy environment for our church family. When you think about a marriage there is equality, yet one head. One husband and one wife—equal in God's sight, yet the husband has the God-given role of being the head of that marriage and family. It works the same way in our church.

Many years ago, when my husband and I began to think about our roles in the church through the metaphor of a healthy family, we had an epiphany moment as we discussed this obvious concept. Most people would agree that a two-parent home is the best-case scenario for children when both parents are healthy. Why would it be any different for a church family? A male senior pastor leads many church families and his wife is often in the shadows somewhere or not involved at all. Would those church families be healthier or more well-balanced if "both parents," the "spiritual dad and mom," were actively involved in loving, teaching, training, raising and caring for the church family?

Along these lines, we found practical encouragement and application for both our home life and church family from Proverbs 1:8, *"Listen, my son, to your father's instruction and do not forsake your mother's teaching." (NIV)*

In the same way that we as parents share the God-given responsibility for managing our home and teaching our children, we operate in leading and teaching the church. In our family and church life, we operate as equals, submitting to one another in love, and yet flowing within the Biblical authority and structure for leadership God has established within marriage. My husband is the head and final authority in our family and our church, but at the same time, he invites, expects, and welcomes my input and insights.

We believe these are our God-given roles. He knows it. I know it. Our kids know it. Our church knows it. God has blessed us and it's worked!

GOOD MANAGEMENT

I am not the only woman serving in leadership in our church. My husband saw the value of high-capacity women early on. Jeff has been very pro-women in ministry. He has always been intentional in giving other women equal opportunity, along with men, to serve God through leadership, teaching, and preaching roles—if those God-given gifts are demonstrated.

Over the years, Jeff has been criticized for his decision to give me and other women a place at the leadership table, but the fruit we've seen has far exceeded the criticism he has received. The result is that our church culture embraces the practice of men and women working together in leadership, teaching, and preaching capacities in our church. The fruit of Jeff's approach in utilizing both men and women in ministry has been growth, both personal and qualitative. Personal growth in the lives of those he's empowered in ministry, and quantitative numerical growth in a church that is influencing southwest Michigan with the gospel.

Because he sees the value of women in church leadership, many women who otherwise may have been frustrated or forced to squander their gifts and callings have found a place to flourish in our church. He takes this passage in Galatians seriously:

> *"For in Christ Jesus you are all sons of God through faith. For as many [of you] as were baptized into Christ [into a spiritual union and communion with Christ, the Anointed one, the Messiah] have put on (clothed yourselves with) Christ. There is [now no distinction] neither Jew nor Greek, there is neither slave nor free, there is not male and female; for you are all one in Christ Jesus" (Galatians 3:26-28, AMP).*

These days, many pastors are now validating their wives and other women in the church by giving them a place in ministry that is congruent with their gifts and callings of God. It is refreshing to find more and more high-profile women serving in the church world in pastoral, senior, executive, management, teaching, leading and creative roles.

It seems that this has always been God's heart. Let's look at some of God's "preacher girls" as mentioned throughout Scripture. But before we move on to Chapter 7, let's get to know two other women who play significant leadership roles in their churches: *Holly Wagner* and *Colleen Rouse.*

WOMEN LEADERS IN THE CHURCH:

HOLLY WAGNER AND COLLEEN ROUSE

Holly Wagner

Colleen Rouse

HOLLY WAGNER

I had the pleasure of meeting Holly Wagner at the Wave Church's "Devoted Women's Conference" hosted by Pastor Sharon Kelly (another amazing leader), and then again when my husband and I visited Oasis Church in Los Angeles pastored by she and her husband Philip. I told Holly I wish I had met her earlier in life as we had many similarities and her easy-going style made her easy to connect with.

She is a wife, mom, pastor, teacher, author and cancer survivor. She is passionate about seeing women become who God has designed them to be. Through GodChicks, the women's ministry of Oasis, and the annual GodChicks conference, Holly encourages thousands of women to understand their value, deepen their relationship with God and have fun on this journey of life.

As you read her profile, I know you will find many similarities with your own experience and be greatly encouraged! Here's Holly:

At one time, Holly Wagner thought she wanted to be a doctor and had medical school in her sights; that is until she took an acting class and got involved in the drama department in college! She discovered she had a love for theatre and doors began to open for her. Through a series of events, she found an agent and landed a role in a television show that took her to Los Angeles. At that point, she said goodbye to organic chemistry and dreams of medical school for good!

Once she got to LA, she met Philip, got plugged into the Bible study he was leading and they fell in love. During this time, while she loved her new life and acting, Holly's heart began to change and she decided that instead of entertaining people, she wanted to help people. She walked away from acting to follow what turned out to be God's call on her life.

In 1984, Holly and Philip officially started Oasis Church and they have worked together as the mom and dad of Oasis from the beginning. Over the years, Holly's role evolved. Initially, she did whatever was needed—whether it was in kids ministry, greeting at the door, teaching classes or providing pastoral care. Holly said,

> "One thing I didn't do was lead worship—I can't sing two notes in the same key! I did whatever was needed. I didn't have to demand a place in our church. As I taught classes, Philip recognized the teaching gift God had given me and he made a way for those gifts to flourish at Oasis. The other thing that became evident was Holly's God-given leadership gift, Both Philip and I recognized that I had a leadership gift and he wanted me to have more of a voice in the direction of the church by serving on the executive team and our vision team."

Philip wasn't the only one who recognized God's calling on Holly's life, others saw those same gifts and she began to receive invitations to travel and teach the Word around the world. These days, Holly speaks at Oasis every four to six weeks and when she's not at Oasis, she can be found traveling and speaking somewhere in the world every weekend.

Has Holly faced any challenges in ministry? Sure, a few! Fortunately, because of the church culture they have created at Oasis, Holly and the role she carries have been embraced and celebrated. That's made her role easy at Oasis, but she understands that's not the way it is for many women in ministry.

Since the early years, most people have known Oasis as the church that Philip and Holly pastor.

> *"If people attend our church and question my role on the platform, it doesn't take them long to realize my role is not going to change, so if they have a problem with women in leadership in ministry, they usually leave and we are okay with that—after all, there are plenty of other churches in LA!"*

In working together with her husband, Holly said,

> *"We both bring our unique perspectives. I am a strong and energetic personality and I can make decisions quickly. Philip is more methodical, deliberate and planned out in his approach, so we have to continually figure out the lanes we run in. We will often have conversations, 'Holly this is your lane. Phillip this is your lane,' to be sure we are on track. We are ever evolving and we have to stay flexible."*

Los Angeles is the perfect place for Holly Wagner. Her raw, real and non-churchy style connects with the diverse, secular and innovative people who are a part of Oasis.

When asked what she would say to the next generation of women who feel called to ministry in the church, Holly said,

> *"I would encourage them to relax, don't try to figure out your whole life. Just take the steps this day needs you to take. Rather than trying to figure out what your future looks like, just look at what's in your hand right now. Use what you have in your hand and do it well. Don't be demanding, be gracious and see what God does with what you have. The other thing I would tell young girls is this: your*

relationships will determine the direction of your life, so choose your friends wisely. For example, is the guy you're dating a friend to your destiny—or a distraction? The people you surround yourself with will make a huge difference in your life."

I asked Holly, knowing what she knows now, what she would say to the Holly of twenty years ago. She replied,

"I would have said, 'Buy the eye cream, you're going to need it!' No, really, I would say 'relax and be who you are!' We wasted several years trying to be other people. We were building a church culture we didn't like—and we wouldn't attend! So, one day, we looked at each other and just decided to be ourselves—that's when we relaxed and changed up our church style and then our church exploded. The other thing I would have said is, 'Love God and ditch those pantyhose!'

The last thing I would say to women of all ages is this: Let's just be like the Proverbs 31 woman! She was a virtuous woman, which means she was a force on earth! I see her life focused on three things: people, means and resources. That means, she knows how to build relationships. She knows how to make money and spend it. She knows how to grow. She's not lazy. She was learning, listening, studying, reading and increasing her capacity as a leader. Don't sit back or passively wait on others, take charge of your own life and go for it!"

Holly's down-to-earth personality, along with the wisdom that comes from her experience in ministry, makes it easy to see why God is using her to lead thousands of people who are a part of Oasis Church, GodChicks and churches around the world.

She's a fabulous role model for women leaders of all ages, and someone worth following!

You can connect with Holly at:

Twitter and Instagram: hollywagnerla

Web: www.oasisla.org or www.GodChicks.com

COLLEEN ROUSE

I am pleased to introduce you to Colleen Rouse. My husband and I went to Bible School with Colleen and her husband, Dennis, in the mid-1980s. We all lived in the same townhouse complex and talked about our ministry dreams at the pool one day.

Twenty-five years later, Dennis and Colleen lead Victory World Outreach a growing mega-church that is changing thousands of lives each week. Together, they pioneered Victory World Church in 1990 after receiving an unmistakable word from God to start a church that would bridge the gap among various cultures and ethnic groups in the Metro Atlanta area. From the very beginning, their dream has been to develop a church that would impact the world.

Today that dream is a reality, and Victory is a thriving multicultural congregation committed to cultural reconciliation, building families, transforming community, and impacting the world. More than 10,000 people from 100+ nations attend Victory each weekend, where Pastors Dennis & Colleen minister on a regular basis. The Rouse's top priority is to remain committed to the Lord. They are also committed to their adult daughter, Lauren, and have been happily married for 30+ years.

I love Colleen's hear for the Lord and ministry! I appreciate the unique leadership and teaching gifts God has given Colleen. She is an encourager and a creative visionary who is full of God's Word and His amazing grace. The Lord is using her and Dennis to influence their church and impact generations, cities, regions, states and nations. I consider it an incredible honor to call this amazing woman of God—my friend! As you read Colleen's story, I know you will be inspired in your own calling.

I distinctly remember sensing a "call" on my life when I was in third grade while attending a parochial school in Pennsylvania. In that moment, even as a child, I began to play out the scenario in my mind. My future would consist of becoming a nun, moving to Africa and subsequently dying of malaria. At least that was my understanding at the time, based on the opportunities I reasoned were available to me as a girl. Even though the outcome wasn't exactly favorable, I recall resigning myself to accept it because it was my assignment. As the years continued, that sense of calling became a distant memory as the desire to be married superseded the desire to become a nun.

Fast forward to my early twenties as I became a born-again believer and the hunger to know this marvelous Savior began to consume me. My soon-to-be husband, Dennis, led me to the Lord and shared my fervency. We found ourselves spending more and more time ministering to hurting people, living on the streets during the week, and teaching in children's ministry on the weekends. For us, it was never an aspiration to be in ministry that fueled us, but a sincere gratitude for being delivered out of darkness that compelled us to take more of an active role in proclaiming the Good News. Shortly after our wedding, the pastor of our young and growing church approached us about starting a youth ministry to the teens. It was in those days that once again the call was awakened, only this time my options were so much greater, or so I thought.

You see, as a former Catholic, in those early years I was opening up the Scriptures and discovering for the first time incredible life-altering truth, which I found to be both liberating and challenging. As a newly engaged woman, I recall reading Paul's admonition to remain unmarried and wondering whether becoming a wife would be going against God's will. In addition, I struggled with what I presumed Paul to say regarding the role of women in ministry, as he seemed to emphasize the importance of a woman's silence in the church. I had to reconcile the sense of my calling and desire to preach God's Word with the things I felt Paul was saying I could not do. I would learn later not to interpret Scripture in a vacuum and come to understand the particular state of the early church and the underlying reasons for the counsel Paul was giving. I would come to learn that Paul was not against marriage any more than he was against women in ministry, and that his main point of commanding silence was to bring order to a service, not to disqualify an entire gender from ministry. I would also learn to allow God to remove any stereotypical lens from my eyes as I attempted to interpret His Word.

I had the blessing of the leadership of the church and my husband, yet the nagging question remained. Of course, it is advisable to allow Scripture to interpret Scripture. I am so thankful for the guidance the Lord gave me to help dismiss my hesitation from fulfilling the calling He gave me. There it was in Acts 18:20 giving an account of a husband and wife team who encounter Apollos, an eloquent teacher of Scripture: "So he began to speak boldly in the synagogue. When Aquila and Priscilla heard him, they took him aside and explained to him the way of God more accurately" (NKJV). It was as if the words jumped off the page in affirming my calling. This was the same author who said that a woman should not teach a man, clearly in support of what had just taken place. Here, a woman alongside her husband was teaching and leading a man, and a leader in the church at that! To me, the precedent was set in that if I, as a woman, have something in the way of truth to offer a brother in the Lord, under the covering and alongside my husband, it was right and good that I serve in this capacity. This was the freedom I needed to move forward.

Today, I am thankful for the encouragement I have received from the Holy Spirit, His Word and many wonderful male leaders who support my desire to fulfill the call. I have also had my share of experiences with those who do not endorse my role. I have watched some vacate their seats and walk out as I open the Word to preach. I've had many interesting opportunities to debate the issue with both men and women, whom I usually encourage to speak with my husband, as I feel no need to defend *myself. One of the more interesting confrontations I received several years ago was from a young woman dressed in a full length blue jean skirt, long hair pulled into a bun and her beautiful face completely devoid of makeup. The reason I mention her appearance is because usually in our day and age, that type of dress is indicative of a conservative stream of the Body of Christ. I took that into account as she explained her struggle with the fact that she loved my message, but just hated that I was preaching it. I tried to comfort her by telling her that just because the word came from the lips of a female, it was not tainted and I encouraged her to not allow the enemy to rob her of the precious truth she had just heard. She walked away, only to return a few moments later and place something into my hand. She said that she was still struggling, but she wanted me to have this anyway. Later, I discovered that she had given me close to $1000 dollars. I remember thinking how interesting it was that clearly she gave with great liberty, but was challenged in her liberty to receive.*

In 30 years of ministry, I have resolved myself to one thing. We are all running a race, as Paul highlights for us. Each of us has been given a lane to run in. As I see it, I cannot allow anyone to push me out of my lane if I am to finish my race in a manner which brings glory to my Saviour. He is the joy that is set before me, along with the expectation of hearing Him say, "Well done, My daughter." The hope of hearing those words of affirmation are all I need to keep running!

Feel free to connect with Colleen Rouse at:

www.twitter.com/colleenrouse

www.instagram.com/cwrouse

Chapter 7

PREACHER GIRLS

When Jesus came on the scene, He did something radical. He talked to women! He included women. He honored women. He called women to help Him preach the gospel.

As we've discovered, women were not widely received as leaders or teachers in the culture of the Old and New Testament times. That's evident by the small number of women leaders, teachers and preachers mentioned in the Bible.

Thankfully, Jesus changed that!

Let's look at the few women leaders, preachers and teachers who are highlighted.

LADY WISDOM

It's interesting that the Book of Proverbs personifies Wisdom as a woman. She, wisdom, cries out, raises her voice, and calls. She is profitable, precious, pleasant and peaceful. She is a tree of life. Lady Wisdom is a leader and a preacher!

AQUILA AND PRISCILLA

Aquila and Priscilla worked together as a ministry team. They are the original pastoral "power-couple," and are always mentioned as a couple.

> *"After these things Paul departed from Athens and went to Corinth.* **And he found a certain Jew named Aquila, born in Pontus, who had recently come from Italy with his wife Priscilla** *(because Claudius had commanded all the Jews to depart from Rome); and he came to them. So, because he was of the same trade, he stayed with them and worked; for by occupation they were tentmakers"* (Acts 18:1-3, NKJV, emphasis mine).

> *"Now a certain Jew named Apollos, born at Alexandria, an eloquent man and mighty in the Scriptures, came to Ephesus. This man had been instructed in the way of the Lord; and being fervent in spirit, he spoke and taught accurately the things of the Lord, though he knew only the baptism of John. So he began to speak boldly in the synagogue.* **When Aquila and Priscilla heard him, they took him aside and explained to him the way of God more accurately"** (Acts 18:24-26, NKJV, emphasis mine).

> **"Greet Priscilla and Aquila, my fellow workers in Christ Jesus,** *who risked their own necks for my life, to whom not only I give thanks, but also all the churches of the Gentiles. Likewise greet the church that is in their house"* (Romans 16:3-5, NKJV, emphasis mine).

"The churches of Asia greet you. *Aquila and Priscilla* greet you heartily in the Lord, *with the church that is in their house*" (1 Corinthians 16:19, NKJV, emphasis mine).

Priscilla's role was as influential as her husband's role, and she is mentioned by name. It appears that they both taught the Word, pastored a church in their home, and labored with the Apostle Paul. We see their influence as a couple extended to many of the churches Paul pioneered.

The International Standard Bible Encyclopedia says,

"Priscilla is equally gifted with her husband as an expounder of 'the way of God,' and instructor of Apollos (Acts 18:26), and as Paul's 'fellow-worker in Christ,' (Romans 16:3)."[1]

Unger's Bible tells us this about Priscilla,

"She seems to have been in full accord with her husband in sustaining the 'church that is in their house' (1 Corinthians 16:19), in helping the apostle Paul (Acts 18:18), and in the theological teaching of Apollos (v. 26)."[2]

Greek Scholar, Kenneth Wuest writes,

"Paul met Prisca the wife, and Aquilla, her husband, first at Corinth. They were tentmakers, and he stayed with them and made tents for a living and at the same time preached the gospel (Acts 18:1-3). The wife's name is given first, because she was the

more prominent Christian worker."[3]

PHOEBE

Paul mentions Phoebe as a deaconess of the church of Cenchrea.

> *"I commend to you **Phoebe our sister, who is a servant of the church in Cenchrea**, that you may receive her in the Lord in a manner worthy of the saints, and assist her in whatever business she has need of you; for indeed she has been a helper of many and of myself also"* (Romans 16:1-2, NKJV, emphasis mine).

Phoebe was actively involved in a strategic role in the church in Cenchrea. In this verse, the word "helper" is translated as "succouror" in the King James Version. This is a word of distinction and leadership. Phoebe was highly regarded in ministry and others were encouraged to assist her in her ministry business.

Vine's Greek Dictionary gives us this definition of succourer or helper:

> *"It is a word of dignity, evidently chosen instead of others which might have been used and indicates the high esteem with which she was regarded, as one who had been a protectress of many. Prostates was the title of a citizen in Athens, who had the responsibility of seeing to the welfare of resident aliens who were without civic rights. Among the Jews it signified a wealthy patron of the community."[4]*

Thayer's Greek Lexicon defines "succourer" as

". . . properly, a woman set over others; a female guardian, protectress, or patroness caring for the affairs of others and aiding them with her resources." [5]

The International Standard Bible Encyclopedia tells us,

"From the first, women held official positions of influence in the church. Phoebe (Romans 16:1) was evidently a deaconess, whom Paul terms 'a servant of the church,' 'a helper of many' and of himself also. Those women who 'labored with me in the Gospel,' (Philippians 4:3) undoubtedly participated with him in preaching." [6]

TRYPHENA, TRYPHOSA, AND PERSIS

"Greet Tryphena and Tryphosa, who have labored in the Lord. Greet the beloved Persis, who labored much in the Lord" (Romans 16:12, NKJV).

Tryphena and Tryphosa were known to be twin sisters recognized for their ministry.

Adam Clarke's Commentary says this about these women:

Two holy women, who it seems were assistants to the apostle in his work, probably by exhorting, visiting the sick, etc. Persis was another woman, who it seems excelled the preceding; for, of her it is said, she "laboured much in the Lord". We learn from this, that Christian women, as well as men, laboured in the ministry of the word. In those times of simplicity all persons, whether men or women, who had received the knowledge of the truth, believed it to be their duty to propagate it to the uttermost of their power. Many have spent much useless labour in endeavouring to prove that these women did not preach. That there were some prophetesses, as well as prophets in the Christian church, we learn; and that a woman might pray or prophesy, provided she had her head covered, we know; and that whoever prophesied spoke unto others to edification, exhortation, and comfort, Paul declares in 1 Cor 14:3. And that no preacher can do more, every person must acknowledge; because to edify, exhort, and comfort, are the prime ends of the Gospel ministry. If women thus prophesied, then women preached. . . [7]

MARY

"Greet Mary, who labored much for us" (Romans 16:6, NKJV).

We aren't certain which Mary this verse refers to, but we do know that she was no slacker. She worked hard in the ministry with Paul.

JUNIA

"Greet Andronicus and Junia, my relatives who have been in prison with me. They are outstanding among the apostles, and they were in Christ before I was" (Romans 16:7, NIV).

Junia and her husband, Andronicus, were apostles. Matthew

Henry's commentary brings this out:

> *Concerning Andronicus and Junia, v. 7. Some take*
> *them for a man and his wife, and the original will*
> *well enough bear it; and, considering the name of the*
> *latter, this is more probable than that they should*
> *be two men, as others think, and brethren. Observe*
> *... (3.) They were of note among the apostles, not so*
> *much perhaps because they were persons of estate*
> *and quality in the world as because they were*
> *eminent for knowledge, and gifts, and graces, which*
> *made them famous among the apostles, who were*
> *competent judges of those things, and were endued*
> *with a spirit of discerning not only the sincerity, but*
> *the eminency, of Christians ...* [8]

EUODIA AND SYNTYCHE

> *"I implore Euodia and I implore Syntyche to be of*
> *the same mind in the Lord. And I urge you also, true*
> *companion, **help these women who labored with***
> ***me in the gospel,** with Clement also, and the rest*
> *of my fellow workers, whose names are in the Book*
> *of Life"* (Philippians 4:2-3, NKJV, emphasis mine).

These women were leaders in the church at Philippi. Anytime you get strong—and even Spirit-filled—women leaders working together there is bound to be some drama from time to time. Their influence was significant enough that Paul addressed their strife in this letter.

PHILIP'S DAUGHTERS

"On the next day we who were Paul's companions departed and came to Caesarea, and entered the house of Philip the evangelist, who was one of the seven, and stayed with him. **Now this man had four virgin daughters who prophesied**" (Acts 21:8-9, NKJV, emphasis mine).

These four girls were preachers! They spoke as they were inspired by the Holy Spirit to give a message.

Adam Clarke's Commentary says:

"Probably these were no more than teachers in the church: for we have already seen that this is a frequent meaning of the word prophesy; and this is undoubtedly one thing intended by the prophecy of Joel, quoted Joel 2:17-18. If Philip's daughters might be prophetesses, why not teachers?"[9]

ANNA

"There was also a prophetess, Anna, the daughter of Phanuel, of the tribe of Asher. She was very old; she had lived with her husband seven years after her marriage, and then was a widow until she was eighty-four. She never left the temple but worshiped night and day, fasting and praying. Coming up to them at that very moment, she gave thanks to God and spoke about the child to all who were looking forward to the redemption of Jerusalem" (Luke 2:36-38, NIV).

Anna was a prophetess, a praying woman and one who

proclaimed and taught others the truth about God.

LOIS AND EUNICE

Timothy's mother and grandmother taught the Bible.

"I have been reminded of your sincere faith, which first lived in your grandmother Lois and in your mother Eunice and, I am persuaded, now lives in you also" (2 Timothy 1:5, NIV).

The International Standard Bible Encyclopedia states,

"To no women did the great apostle feel himself more deeply indebted than to Lois and Eunice, grandmother and mother of Timothy, whose 'faith unfeigned' and ceaseless instructions from the holy Scriptures (2 Timothy 1:5; 3:14-15) gave him the most 'beloved child' and assistant in his ministry. Their names have been conspicuous in Christian history for maternal love, spiritual devotion, and fidelity in teaching the Word of God."[10]

MIRIAM AND DEBORAH

God called and anointed women to leadership in the Old Testament. It's interesting to note that Miriam, a woman and prophetess, was the first person called to lead worship in the Old Testament. God set Miriam in leadership along with Moses and Aaron.

"For I brought you up from the land of Egypt, I redeemed you from the house of bondage; and I sent before you Moses, Aaron, and Miriam" (Micah 6:4, NKJV).

Deborah served in a senior leader role. We see her story in Judges 4. She was a prophetess and judge. She judged Israel and her reign gives us the first instance of a female-led government. She was a senior leader in both civil and religious arenas. In addition, Deborah gave direction and assignments to men. She appointed Barak to be the general of the armies as the chief ruler. Her husband Lapidoth appears to be supportive, but uninvolved in leadership. God anointed and blessed Deborah.

OTHER WOMEN IN THE BIBLE AND MODERN HISTORY

In the Old Testament, we see God's hand on numerous other women including Esther and Huldah for leadership and teaching others.

The International Standard Bible Encyclopedia says:

> *"Women, as well as men, took upon themselves the self-renouncing vow of the Nazarite (Numbers 6:2), and shared in offering sacrifices, as in the vow and sacrifice of Manoah's wife (Judges 13:13-14); were granted theophanies, e.g. Hagar (Genesis 16:7; 21:17), Sarah (Genesis 18:9-10), Manoah's wife (Judges 13:3-5,9); were even permitted to 'minister' at the door of the sanctuary (Exodus 38:8; 1 Samuel 2:22); rendered conspicuous service in national religious songs and dances (Exodus 15:20; Judges 11:34; 1 Samuel 18:6-7). They shared equally with men in the great religious feasts, as is indicated by the law requiring their attendance (Deuteronomy 12:18)."*[11]

History records more women leaders, preachers and teachers than you might imagine. Many women walked in the light and revelation they had at the time—at times with the approval and encouragement of their husbands and often the disapproval and discouragement of those who did not believe in women preachers. Let's look at the roster.

Susanna Wesley, mother of ten children including John and Charles Wesley, felt God's call to do more for the Lord in addition to mothering ten children. She told her husband, *"It came into my mind that though I am not a man nor a minister of the Gospel, and so cannot be employed in such a worthy employment as they were, yet if my heart were sincerely devoted to God, and if I were inspired with a true zeal for His glory and did really desire the salvation of souls, I might do something more than I do."* She turned her Sunday family worship time into an evening service that 200 people attended regularly.[12]

Catherine Booth, the wife of William Booth, founder of the Salvation Army, worked in tandem with her husband much like Aquilla and Priscilla in preaching and writing. In her first published article in *The Connexion Magazine*, she pointed out that "women were last at the Cross and first at the sepulcher." She went on later to say, *"I believe it is impossible to estimate the extent of the Church's loss, where prejudice and custom are allowed to render the outpouring of God's spirit upon His handmaidens null and void."* She authored half a dozen books and when she died at 61, all of England mourned and 50,000 people filed past her coffin. [13]

Hannah Whitall Smith was a well known Quaker and known for her devotional classic of 1875, *The Christian's Secret of a Happy Life*, which by 1950 sold over two million copies and had been translated into many languages. She and her husband Robert Pearsall Smith were prominent in founding the Keswick Movement. She preached regularly and her success was equal to her husband's. [14]

Charles G. Finney, the revivalist, gave prominence to the place of women. As a Professor of Theology at Oberlin College, he insisted that Scripture did not prohibit the speaking or praying of women in mixed assemblies. [15]

W.B. Godbey, a holiness preacher, wrote a pamphlet in 1891 titled, "Woman Preacher" and said, *"It is a God-given right, blood-bought privilege, and bounden duty of the women, as well as the men, to preach the gospel."* Regarding the verse, "It is a shame for a woman to speak in the church," Godbey said this was given to keep order, not to keep women from preaching. He went on to say; *"I don't know a scripture in all the Bible by whose perversion the devil has dragged more souls into hell than this."*[16]

History is loaded with stories of both well-known and unknown women who blazed trails as they preached the gospel, led people to Christ, trained disciples, started movements, overcame persecution and mockery and put a dent in eternity.

TODAY'S PREACHER GIRLS

In looking back, it's easy to see God's calling and anointing upon women of the Bible as well as those in our recent history. Their fruit speaks for itself. In fact, we might wonder, if God was as displeased with these woman leaders and preachers as some would expect Him to be, you'd think it would be evidenced by a lack in anointing and fruit. Instead, these faithful women produced great fruit that had a legacy-leaving impact.

> *Jesus said, "By their fruit you will recognize them. Do people pick grapes from thornbushes, or figs from thistles? Likewise, every good tree bears good fruit, but a bad tree bears bad fruit. A good tree cannot bear bad fruit, and a bad tree cannot bear good fruit. Every tree that does not bear good fruit is cut down and thrown into the fire. Thus, by their fruit you will recognize them" (Matthew 7:16-20, NIV).*

What about you, preacher girl? Are you stirred up by reading the stories of other faithful women? Is God calling you? Is His Word like a fire shut up in your bones? Do you want to maximize your life for His purposes? Does your heart long to lead, teach, preach and produce eternal fruit? You are in good company!

Remember what Jesus said, *"You did not choose me, but I chose you and appointed you to go and bear fruit—fruit that will last" (John 15:16, NIV).*

Let the fruit speak.

CHAPTER 8

WHO'S REALLY BEHIND THE GREAT SILENCE?

Journal Entry: *"So, I am at this conference...I am the only woman seated at the rich glossy black conference table in a room full of pastors—make that 24 male senior pastors. I scanned the room and made assumptions—average age 39; ministry experience seven years. And then, there's Jeff and me.*

I could tell I wasn't invited. We were all seated snuggly at the conference and gazing in the direction of the ringleader—the church growth guru—he is handsome, strong, successful, humble and deliberate. It was obvious—this was his rodeo and we were there to learn.

I had been excited and so expectant until this moment. Suddenly, I felt all the eyes in the room focusing on me when the guru reminded everyone that this special session was just for senior pastors and he was sorry there just wasn't room for spouses. In other words, spouses should really not be in this room right now—especially the woman spouse that was living in my body. I tried not to turn red, I felt the blood moving up my neck and I tried to push it down, but there it went—my face was definitely red. I tried to maintain my, "It's all good people, really, I am supposed to be here," look.

After all, I was a senior pastor...and I was a spouse. Jeff wanted me to join him in this meeting. He and I had been working together as a husband/wife team pastoral team—like Aquila and Priscilla in the Bible—for over two decades. Our little start up church in Kalamazoo had grown from five adults to thousands. We believed God authorized it. My husband validated it and I had the fruit and the scars to prove my role and this calling.

But unfortunately by the definition of the nice guru and the other senior pastors in the room, I didn't qualify. One simple reason: I was a girl. That's the reason everything got funky in that conference room: girls can't be leaders—definitely not senior leaders—in churches. Sure, girls can be CEOs, Supreme Court Justices, governors, senators, brain surgeons, prime ministers and astronauts, but girls cannot be church leaders.

I sat there feeling like any value, worth, fruit or dignity I thought I had ten minutes before I walked into that conference room, was being sucked right out of me. I had to sit there like some reject who was probably completely rebelling against her husband, wearing the pants, being a Jezebel and who didn't know her place in life. I hated this feeling of being dismissed, minimized, overlooked, rejected, devalued and uninvited. But I sat there. I listened. I smiled. I pretended to take notes. Other than that, I didn't move a muscle. I went stealth. Invisible.

You'd think after years of pastoring and buckets of fruit, we'd be past these funky-town moments. Up until this time, I had been as excited about ministry as I was when we started. But things like this had happened so many times over the years, I was tired of the demeaning treatment and questions. "Do you do anything around here?" "I don't believe in women preachers, we're leaving." "How can you teach, when the Bible says women are to be silent?" "This conference is only for men...the ladies are going shopping." Geeze louize!

Why the heck was the church world so far behind? Why did they want to silence 50% of their potential human resources? How was it possible, that somewhere along the way, church leaders had taken two verses out of their cultural context and overlooked dozens of others to make sure women had no role in the leadership of a local church?

There I was in a full-blown pity party, when all of the sudden, the slack was jerked out of me and a light bulb turned on. Wait a minute?! My struggle is not against flesh and blood! It wasn't the church or the men in the conference room who wanted to minimize me and silence 50% of the population...it was the enemy!

And that really fired me up!

After all, when you think about it, why *is* such a mountain being made out of a molehill? Why *is* a big deal made about a woman's role in the church? Why all the controversy over women as preachers, pastors, Bible teachers or church leaders?

Why are we still even talking about this topic?

Then, it became even more obvious. Without over-spiritualizing things, who has a motive for silencing women? Who benefits?

> *Who really wants to silence half of the Christian population?*

> *Who really doesn't want the gospel or the Word to go forth?*

SATAN'S WORST NIGHTMARE

The devil has a motive. The devil receives benefits.

Satan's worst nightmare is an army of men *and* women who are teaching, preaching, proclaiming, declaring and prophesying the Word of God! After all, research has shown that women have a need to speak three times as many words a day as men![1] What would happen if millions of women who love to talk were turned loose to preach, teach, and lead?

> *The thought probably makes hell tremble!*

This sort of sounds like Psalm 68:11 doesn't it? *"The Lord gives the word [of power];* **the women who bear and publish [the news] are a great host**" (AMP, emphasis mine).

Perhaps, we do need to reconsider the enemy and his strategies. After the fall of man, the Lord forewarned us about the devices of the evil one: *"And I will put enmity between you and the woman"* (Genesis 3:15, NKJV). Obviously, there has been enmity between the devil and the Seed of woman, Jesus Christ. To another degree, there has been enmity between women as a gender and the evil one, as well. It's very likely that one of his tactical moves and strategic devices has been to create this confusion and controversy about the role of women in the church. While we debate it, has he effectively silenced fifty percent of the Body of Christ?

What could happen to Satan's kingdom if women and men worked together—in unity and love—to lead, teach and preach the gospel to this lost and dying world?

It's an exciting thought!

BALANCE

Before you put on your camo and buckle up your combat boots ladies, let's talk about balance. There are always extremes in everything God desires for His church. This area is no exception.

One ditch is the idea that women should take over and dominate in the church—sort of a Christian version of the Women's Liberation Movement. God's Word absolutely does not advocate that! The other ditch is that women are to be subservient doormats that have no place in the leadership, teaching, or preaching of the church. We have seen from looking into God's Word that this view is not supported in Scripture.

Jesus set women free.

However, Jesus does not condone women who resort to an arrogant persona with a rebellious, resentful, men-hating spirit, rather He empowers us to be wise and gracious women, wives, moms, leaders, preachers, teachers, and servants who help Him and the men in our lives build His Church!

One of the best and all time classic passages about a balanced, godly woman is found in Proverbs 31.

She was some lady!

She is the ideal Christian woman. She's got it together. She loves God. She loves her husband. She's a great wife and mom. Her kids love her. She's a strong leader who is successful in business enterprises and ministry. She's influential. She's a good friend. She's fun, kind, wise, and bold. Her priorities are in the right place. She has it going on! The best thing about her is that everything about her life stems from her walk with God. If you haven't done so lately, be sure to read about the Proverbs 31 woman; she's a great person to study and imitate.

10 REALITY CHECKS

Ladies, I hope you have you been encouraged by reading this book. I pray you are fired up, revived and ready to pursue the calling and the dreams God has put in your heart!

While you are getting ready to stomp on the devil's head, let's take a moment to do a reality check. Just because you read this book and are ready to run, doesn't mean it will be a piece of cake. So, let's get prepared for a few realities.

1. **People Aren't the Enemy.** When you face critics and naysayers, just remember: your struggle is not against flesh and blood. You do have an enemy—it's the devil. People are not the enemy. So, don't allow yourself to get mad or frustrated by people. The devil is the one who wants 50% of the population silenced. God's Word is your weapon.

2. **Walk in Love.** Everyone won't be as excited as you are about the role of women in the church. They haven't read the book or gotten the tee shirt. They may be stuck in traditions and old ways of thinking. Some people will still disagree and reject you for being a woman in leadership. That's life and the sooner you accept it, the better. Just be sweet and preach on! Walk in love and do what God has called you to do. *"He who calls you is faithful, who also will do it"* (1 Thessalonians 5:24, NKJV).

3. **Family First.** Don't get hyper-spiritual or so ministry minded that you forget about your first ministry—your family! Finding balance, pursuing your dreams, and juggling everything on your plate is not always easy, so talk with your husband and kids and decide what type of schedule or priorities will work best for your family in the various seasons of life.

4. **Don't Force It.** I like what Pastor Ed Young says to people in ministry, "Let the game come to you." As a woman, you don't have to act like a man or force your way into anything. Don't be a lone ranger. Don't build your

own kingdom. Love God and love people. Stay hooked up to your local church—the house where God has you planted. Seek counsel and confirmation about the use of your gifts and—and God's timing—from your pastor and the other godly men and women in your life. Rest in His calling and anointing. Your gifts will make a way for you—and He will bring the game to you.

5.   Faithfulness Counts. Go ahead and get started being faithful in small things in your local church. You won't start where you will end up. Your "ministry assignments" might include a lengthy stint cleaning the church bathrooms, volunteering in kids church or bringing that chicken divan casserole to a few funerals— before you're preaching to stadiums! God is not in the business of raising up "flash in the pan" superstars. He sees the big, eternal picture. Often, He allows His Word to work in us for years, even decades, to develop the foundation of character and maturity that will be needed for the ministry He wants to build through us. When He counts us faithful, He puts us in the ministry. *"And I thank Christ Jesus our Lord who has enabled me, because He counted me faithful, putting me into the ministry"* (1Timothy 1:12, NKJV).

6.   One Bad Apple Can Spoil the Whole Bunch of Girls. Unfortunately, some church leaders have had bad experiences with women leaders in the church, whether in worship ministry, student ministries, prayer meetings, small groups or women's ministry. The result is that women are often guilty of and/or perceived as being too critical, ego-driven, emotional, over-eager or hyper-spiritual and their behavior often does damage to the church. Pastors and church leaders on the receiving end of this type of behavior are very reluctant to trust women leaders. If you are serving someone who's had a bad experience with other women in ministry, you will have to spend some extra time proving that you are trustworthy and credible. It's not fair, but it is a reality.

7.   This Isn't a Perfect World. In a perfect world, it's probably best for a husband and wife to serve together as lead or senior pastors. While there will be some criticism, they will face less criticism than a woman who takes on the sole role of senior pastor. If you are a woman who feels called to go solo as you start, plant or pastor a church, you will probably face more opposition than anyone. Your best bet is to reach out to people far from God—seek people who are lost as can be and full of hurt and pain—they aren't religious and don't know anything about the "woman preacher" controversy. They will be thrilled to see you coming as they are hungry to experience God's love, hope and a new life.

8.   Don't Debate It—Just Build It. While the enemy will stir up people to push your buttons and lure you into a debate about the role of women in the church, don't go there. Don't debate the topic, just build the church! The best way to overcome the devil when he tries to discourage you is to live out your calling by faith. Don't quit. Join forces with Jesus. Follow His favor and He will open all the doors you need!

9.   Let Your Fruit Do the Talking. It might take many years, but at the end of the day, no matter how many critics you have or how many setbacks you face, if you stay steady, eventually people will see the fruit of your life and ministry as impacting eternity and bringing honor and glory to Jesus Christ. It's hard to argue with good, consistent fruit.

10. Don't Compare. That's easier said than done. As women, we often compare ourselves to others and we usually end up on the short end of the stick. The "other" woman is always prettier, smarter, skinnier, funnier, sweeter, more gracious, more stylish, more successful, more anointed and more capable than we'll ever be. If we aren't careful, we'll slide into "auto-loser" mode and allow intimidation and insecurity to rob us of the confidence we need to fulfill God's plan. Don't do it!

SHATTER THAT GLASS

In case you are thinking that you have to be perfect or have the perfect family as you step into leadership in the church, let's shatter some glass with a few stories.

You Are Making a Difference: For you women who wonder if your ministry is making a difference—it probably is, but maybe not in the ways you thought. The fat lady hasn't hit her last note yet, so the verdict about your effectiveness is not in! God measures things differently than we do; it's very likely you are much more fruitful than you realize.

Maybe this will encourage you. After we had been pastoring for about four years, we were feeling pretty good about the growth of the church. I had been encouraged by the spiritual growth I saw in one particular guy in the church who took my "Getting a Grip on the Basics" class. We'll call him Leonard. He had been serving as a lead teacher in our Children's Church, and one day he excitedly stopped by the church to tell our secretary something God had revealed to him. He said that he had asked Jesus what he (Leonard) should get Him (Jesus) for His birthday—for Christmas. Leonard said, "Jesus told me what He wanted for His birthday. He told me to quit smoking pot." Yep! Your reaction was just like ours. Stunned! Then hilarious laughing! We were happy for Leonard, but it was obvious that our work here was not yet done!

Enjoy Those Popped-Balloon Moments: For you women in ministry with young kids—enjoy the moments. It was a great Sunday morning at Valley Family Church. The worship team was having a good day and everyone was enjoying God's Presence. Our son Luke, around eight years old at the time, was standing next to me and I could see his eyes were closed and one of his hands was in the air praising the Lord. I was having a proud mom moment. After a few minutes, he tugged on my sleeve and I thought, *Praise the Lord, I wonder what revelation God has just shown him? Maybe he feels called to the ministry? Maybe he just saw angels on the platform?* I bent low with anticipation to hear Luke's divine revelation. "Mom," Luke said, "can we get a foosball table?" I heard the loud sound of Pop! as I realized the balloon of my proud mom moment just exploded! For the rest of the worship, I laughed. I am sure our worship leader thought I was being overcome with the joy of the Lord from the amazing worship, but by then I was completely out of the spirit. I was just laughing at God's sense of humor and how He gives us a reality check, right when we need it.

Remember, God's Got Your Number: For you older women who've been at it for a while, God hasn't forgotten about you. He's got your number! If you've been disappointed, discouraged and disheartened, it's time to get your chin up, buttercup! God knows all about the challenges you've faced and He knows how to bring you the word of encouragement you need.

A few years ago, after 30 years in ministry, twenty-five years of marriage, four kids, twenty years leading a growing church and authoring around eighteen books that had been translated into over 15 languages, you'd think I would have been way past being seriously discouraged. However, in 2008, we entered an exceptionally stormy season and it seemed like all hell was coming against us as we were building a new church facility on the interstate between Chicago and Detroit. Right in the middle of this, I experienced several big blows that sent me into an unexpected tailspin of discouragement.

First, it was an 18-month non-stop battle with our city and a media circus with nearby neighbors who didn't want our church to be built at all. Then it was a personally devastating season with my dad. After that, it was betrayal from a few people we thought were close friends, and several other unexpected ministry disappointments. All of these might have just been considered "comes with the territory—blips on the radar," but in this season everything piled on and seemed to be amplified. I had to really fight through the enemy's discouragement that tried to sidetrack me.

As this stormy season was coming to an end, God did something that lifted my spirits beyond measure—perhaps this will minister to you, too. At a luncheon we attended, a dear pastor friend whom we had not seen in years, Gerald Brooks, came up to the table Jeff and I were sitting at and said, *"Beth, can I speak with you for a minute? Bring Jeff."* So, Jeff and I got up and met with Gerald just outside the luncheon hall. Gerald said, *"I don't normally do this. I am not one who just 'gives people words,' but the Lord won't let me get away from this. Beth, He wants you to know, 'Man has rejected you, but God approves of you. Don't let that rejection affect you any longer.'"* Those words ministered grace to me in a big way!

Maybe that's what you need to hear today? The devil might be trying to take you out, but let God grace these words for you: *"Man has rejected you, but God approves of you. Don't let that rejection affect you any longer."*

Be encouraged by Psalm 139:1-16 from The Message Bible,

> GOD, *investigate my life; get all the facts firsthand. I'm an open book to you; even from a distance, you know what I'm thinking. You know when I leave and when I get back; I'm never out of your sight. You know everything I'm going to say before I start the first sentence. I look behind me and you're there, then up ahead and you're there, too—your reassuring presence, coming and going. This is too much, too wonderful—I can't take it all in! Is there anyplace I can go to avoid your Spirit? to be out of your sight? If I climb to the sky, you're there! If I go underground, you're there! If I flew on morning's wings to the far western horizon, You'd find me in a*

minute—you're already there waiting! Then I said to myself, "Oh, he even sees me in the dark! At night I'm immersed in the light!" It's a fact: darkness isn't dark to you; night and day, darkness and light, they're all the same to you. Oh yes, you shaped me first inside, then out; you formed me in my mother's womb. I thank you, High God—you're breathtaking! Body and soul, I am marvelously made! I worship in adoration—what a creation! You know me inside and out, you know every bone in my body; You know exactly how I was made, bit by bit, how I was sculpted from nothing into something. Like an open book, you watched me grow from conception to birth; all the stages of my life were spread out before you, The days of my life all prepared before I'd even lived one day.

Before we move on to Chapter 9, let's look at another group of inspiring young women in leadership in the church: *Nicole Crank, Andi Andrew* and *Sarah Wehrli.*

WOMEN LEADERS IN THE CHURCH:

NICOLE CRANK, ANDI ANDREW AND SARAH WEHRLI

Nicole Crank

Sarah Wehrli

Andi Andrew

NICOLE CRANK

I've recently come to know and appreciate Nicole Crank and the unique leadership and teaching gifts God has given her. She's a mover and a shaker...fun and full of vision, energy and passion.

She is the wife of David, mother of Austin and Ashtyn, and the co-founder and senior pastor of Faith Church in St. Louis, Missouri, and West Palm Beach, Florida, recognized by Outreach Magazine as one of the top five fastest growing churches. Nicole hosts numerous "I Am Women" events and writes a popular blog.

She is one of the nation's most heavily sought after inspirational speakers. Her successful background in the corporate world and the ministry has granted her frequent showings on ABC in St. Louis, Missouri, as well as guest appearances on global television networks such as Daystar and TBN. I hope you are as inspired by Nicole as I have been!

YOUR CALL:

Q: How would you describe your call to ministry and the specific role you have in your church?

NC: When I was 24 years old, I was going through a terrible divorce with someone who had gotten involved with drugs. I remember, I was driving and I called my mom and told her that I felt like I was supposed to share my experience with others. I wasn't sure how or when this would happen, but I knew that others could benefit from the trials I had come through. That calling was dormant in me for eight years, until my father-in-law suddenly passed away and my husband and I took over the responsibility of running the church.

I serve in leading, teaching and preaching as senior pastor and executive pastor. I preach to our congregation at least once a month. I, along with my husband David, lead our staff and volunteers.

Q: Have you been reluctant to embrace your call to leadership or teaching in the church?

NC: At first, new things overwhelmed me. I had to rely completely on God. I wanted to do it all well; be a good spouse, mom and pastor.

YOUR CHALLENGES:

Q: What are your thoughts about churches that do not ordain, license or allow women in leadership ministry roles? What experiences and/or responses have you had when you are told that it is not biblical for women to be in ministry or that pastoral ministry is only for males?

NC: My experience has been others have picketed our church for allowing me to speak. Luckily, I wasn't even there at the time. I was speaking at a conference out of town.

I might say that we're never going to see "eye to eye." But if God can use a donkey...I think I'm smarter than a donkey, most days! I think they are missing out on all those special gifts and talents that God purposely sent to help. Many gatherings of pastors invite the men to discussion groups and send the wives shopping. I would rather sit in on the meetings and at least take notes. I know how to be in attendance without having to be heard.

YOUR HUSBAND:

Q: Describe working together as a team with your husband in ministry.

NC: We work together all day every day, and all night. David prays and follows God's direction. He does open doors for me, and often pushes me through them.

Q: Do you ever struggle with not wanting your husband to feel threatened or in competition with you?

NC: Yes. Anytime you have two people doing the same thing, it's important to understand that we're there to complete each other...not compete with each other.

Q: If you could coach a young husband/pastor in how to encourage/release his wife and her gifts in the church, what would you say to him?

NC: Don't try to make her into every other preacher's wife or just fill a space that needs filled in the church. Release her in HER gifts to be what God wants her to be.

YOUR FAMILY:

Q: Are other members of your family involved with you in ministry? Do you have daughters who feel called to leadership or a teaching role in the ministry?

NC: Yes. My son is a youth pastor training to become a campus pastor. My daughter leads worship in the children's ministry every week and is a worship leader in training. She is ten and especially likes to sit in on the planning meetings for our Women's Conference—and she always has some great ideas!

YOUR ROLE:

Q: Have you ever felt like a misfit in ministry and church life?

NC: Yes. Sometimes I tend to think more like a man, and there are women who don't understand that part of me.

Q: Ever wished you could use your gifts to their full potential outside of the church in a secular professional role – instead of inside the church?

NC: Been there...done that! I left the corporate world for the church world.

Q: What percentage would you say you feel in terms of being fulfilled and satisfied in your calling as a woman in leadership in the church?

NC: 110%

To connect with Nicole:

Faithchurch.com

Nicolecrank.com

Instagram: nicolecrank

Twitter: nicolecrank

Facebook: Nicole Filla Crank

ANDI ANDREW

I met Andi Andrew just over a year ago and I could tell she was a powerhouse for God. She is the real deal—passionate, authentic and full of vision. She is most definitely a strong voice impacting this generation for God. I was actually introduced to the effectiveness of Andi's ministry by our young adult daughters, Meghan and Annie, who were fans of Andi before I knew her. They loved listening to her podcasts and were being challenged and inspired by her compelling, down-to-earth messages.

Andi and her husband Paul carry the leadership of Liberty Church in New York City, and she is an outstanding sought-after speaker. Andi's years of ministry have shaped her with a passion to see people experience real freedom, and it's little wonder her leadership and ministry have such a lasting impact. Andi grew up in Spokane, Washington, and met her husband Paul in Bible college in Australia. As well as building the church, she's blessed with four incredible kids...three boys and a little princess. They're not the normal New York family, but they're convinced normal is over-rated anyway.

YOUR CALL:

Q: Describe your call to ministry:

AA: I was 19 years old. The moment I felt "the call" was literally on the alter call where I gave my life to Jesus. I had been in college at the University of Washington the year prior, messing up my life real good, spending thousands of dollars on tuition, and directionless. Then I encountered God in a tangible way and wanted nothing more than to build His Church (whatever that meant and whatever that looked like). I had no pre-conceived ideas about any of it. I fell in love and wanted to give my entire life to the One who saved me and loved me first. I literally said "I'll do anything for You." And from that day forward, I have been.

Q: What is your role in the local church—who, what, when and where do you minister?

AA: I preach at least once a month to our entire church, as well as our Women's Ministry. I serve on our leadership team and anywhere I'm needed. I lead alongside my husband. We lead the entire church together. We are equal, but carry very different roles. He steers the ship and I make sure everyone on the ship is healthy. I administrate the pastoral care within our church to make sure needs are met. Paul lets us know the direction in which the church is going. I lead the women and disciple our key women one-on-one. I also have a huge role on our teaching team. We truly do it all together and are a perfectly matched team.

Q: Have you been reluctant to embrace your call to leadership or teaching in the church?

AA: Not until I moved to NYC and faced opposition for being a women who leads. I had never experienced that before. We as a team have done a deep dive into the theology of women in ministry as we all needed a leg to stand on to move forward as a church. I personally needed a theological foundation to stand on to be able to impart into the hearts and lives of those I am called to.

My husband believes in people no matter their gender, race, or background. I experienced opposition and had negative words spoken against me as I led alongside my husband in New York. People would literally say – "I received from your teaching today, but can't stay at this church because I don't believe in women in ministry," and things like that. I think the hardest part for me was hearing that from another woman. It really shook me and caused me to deeply walk with conviction, whilst seeking out understanding as to why we as a church believe what we believe about women in ministry.

YOUR CHALLENGES:

Q: What has been the biggest challenge for you to overcome as a woman in ministry?

AA: The battlefield of the mind. Not buying into the lies that were spoken over me by negative people about my calling. God made me a woman on purpose...it wasn't a mistake, and I like who I am. I am made in His image, and am secure in that. The only time I get insecure in it is when I believe lies about what others say about me.

Q: What are your thoughts about churches that do not recognize, allow, license or ordain women in leadership ministry roles?

AA: I think we're at a pivotal turning point as the Church, where we all need to have another look at these issues even if the answers surprise us. I know I needed to. The disqualification of 50% of the human race for leadership in the Church is definitely something to take a deeper look at.

Q: What experiences and/or responses have you had when you are told that it is not biblical for women to be in ministry or that pastoral ministry is only for males?

AA: Mainly I've experienced people just spouting their opinion to Paul and me. A lot of times people just want to be right about this issue, and not teachable, because if they're wrong, their whole belief system is messed with. Other times, I've had encounters with people who genuinely desire deeper understanding on the issue.

Q: What would you say to a woman who has been told she cannot minister?

AA: It's a lie. Ministry is "to meet a need," and we are all in ministry. You're constantly ministering to your kids, husband, friends, those in church—you just don't have a title. I would also tell them to be bold and humble, and begin to ask more questions if they feel they are to begin leading, even with young children still in their household. I'm not saying to step out in rebellion. Be led by the Holy Spirit as to how to take each step you feel God is asking you to take for your life. It's not for everyone, but you answer to God at the end of your life for your obedience to Him or your fear of man, when it comes to your specific calling.

YOUR HUSBAND:

Q: Describe the way you and your husband work together as a team.

AA: I think we're both very comfortable in who we are. We are very different and bring different strengths to the table. He gives me opportunities without even thinking, because it's just how we roll.

Q: Do you ever struggle with not wanting your husband to feel threatened or in competition with you?

AA: No. He isn't and has never been threatened by me. It's a huge reason why I fell in love with him.

Q: If you could coach a young husband/pastor in how to encourage/release his wife and her gifts in the church, what would you say to him?

AA: Just let her be who she is. Don't put unrealistic expectations on her, nor compare her to any other woman in or out of ministry that you have seen. There is no "standard" except for what God calls you to as a family. And be patient with her as she wrestles with it. So many factors come into play for us as women. We have so many roles that deeply matter to us: relationship with God, husband, children, leadership, calling, running an awesome household... the list goes on and they all touch each other. We have to wrestle with what it looks like for us as an individual without comparing our race to another. So just cheer her on, speak truth, love, and life over her and watch her flourish in her lane!

To connect with Andi, you can find her here:

www.libertychurchnyc.com

www.andiandrew.com

SARAH WEHRLI

I am excited to introduce you to Sarah Wehrli, one of the next generation's women leaders in the church. Sarah and her husband Caleb are visionaries and pioneers. Sarah is also the author of, *Awake: Rise to Your Divine Assignment.*

Sarah comes from a heritage of faith. She became involved in ministry at an early age as a Pastor's Kid (PK), raised by legendary Pastors Billy Joe and Sharon Daugherty, who founded and pastored Victory Christian Center in Tulsa, Oklahoma. After her father passed on to heaven in 2009, her mother Sharon Daugherty stepped in to lead Victory Christian Center. Her two brothers are also both in pastoral leadership there. Her sister and her husband are church planters in Texas. Sarah and Caleb's own children are young right now, but they still include them in serving areas—helping to pass out fliers, set up church, etc. They are the next generation in Sarah's family helping to build the church!

I had heard great things about Sarah from one of our daughters who had heard her speak at a women's event and enjoyed relating to her as a fellow PK. We recently met Sarah at a global evangelism event and I was instantly impressed with her gracious spirit of faith. She is woman full of compassion and vision, and it will be exciting to see what God does through her and Caleb and Victory Orlando. I know you'll love her profile.

YOUR CALL:

Q: How would you describe your call to ministry?

SW: As an 11 year old, I remember being in a children's church service during worship when I had a vision. In the vision, I was standing with Jesus in front of a huge video screen. Suddenly, pictures of children from all over the world began to flash on the screen. They were hungry, thirsty, alone, and hopeless. I asked Jesus, "Why are You showing me this?" He replied, "Because these are the people I've called you to reach." I said, "But I am only 11."

He reminded me of Jeremiah 1:5-8, when God called Jeremiah and said, "Before I formed you in the womb I knew you, before you were born I set you apart; I appointed you as a prophet to the nations." But Jeremiah replied, "But God, I don't know how to speak, I am only a youth.' And God replied, "Don't say I am only a youth, for you will go to whoever I send you to, and whatever I tell you to say, you will say. Don't be afraid of them for I am with you says the Lord."

After that I knew I was called to the nations to preach the gospel and help hurting children. When I came home, my dad encouraged me to find a regular place in our church I could serve. As the pastor of our church, my dad knew that we needed to share what we were receiving with others. He encouraged me to start helping the inner city children that were bused into our church weekly. As I was involved in loving on those precious children, compassion grew in my heart for those who were lost and without hope.

Another thing God used to help me understand my calling was through leading a Bible study for young girls in our local church. After that I realized one of my passions was to encourage young women in their purpose and calling. I think many times, we discover our calling and gifts as we serve in an area.

Q: What roles have you had in the local church?

SW: When my dad first asked me to be one of the children's pastors over a service, I did not feel capable. I was a young college student, working another part-time job and felt overwhelmed by the task. My dad had asked several other older "experienced" couples to lead the new children's service, but couldn't find anyone. After prayer, He felt he was to ask me to do it. He saw something in me that I didn't see in myself. I had been volunteering for several years, but didn't feel that I measured up to the task. I tried to make excuses but he said, "Sarah, you can do it and your sister Ruthie will help you." He added, "I have asked everyone else and cannot find anyone, so you are it!" Ha! (Any pastor's kid can probably relate).

That experience caused me to grow in my leadership and we saw God do amazing things in those kids. The cool thing was that many of those same children I had in children's church went on to be involved in our youth group when I was moved to be a youth pastor, and then on into young adult ministry where Caleb and I pastored. You could say we all "grew up" together. I praise God that many are still involved in church and ministry today! This is one of the greatest joys as a pastor—to see young men and women you encouraged, making a difference in the world today.

In each new season, when I was asked to take on a new leadership role or speak in the church, one of the things I had to combat was fear because I knew the weight of the responsibility and I didn't want to fail. I am forever thankful that my pastor (my dad) encouraged and challenged me to continue to press into God and give out of myself to others.

Through it all, what strengthens me is keeping my relationship with Jesus a priority, loving those He called me to serve and staying faithful to the assignment He has given me in each season.

I love being involved in ministry. It is an honor to serve the Lord. It has not always been easy and there have been times I have wanted to quit but I wouldn't trade it for anything! I know this is what God has called me to do. I believe giving and serving others has helped me grow as Christian. I started volunteering in areas of the church when I was 12 years old, and then came on as a part-time staff member at our home church when I was 18 years old. While I was in college, I continued to serve part-time and then after graduation, I came on full-time and served there for 13 years before moving overseas. Some of my favorite moments have been ministering to women in other nations who have been devalued and beaten down. I love seeing women encouraged in fulfilling their divine assignment!

Throughout the years, I have been involved in different areas of my home church—serving as a children's pastor, junior high youth pastor, young adult pastor, mission's director, and women's ministry leader. Then in 2008, my husband and I and our two children moved to Hong Kong to do missions work throughout Southeast Asia for two years. We founded Inspire International, a ministry focused on evangelizing and equipping leaders as well as humanitarian aid, such as building orphanages and water wells. During our time living overseas, we served in leadership at a church in Hong Kong and traveled each month to do missions work in surrounding nations. While in Hong Kong, I helped in worship and led women's conferences during that season. When my dad passed away, we moved back to the states to help my mom and our home church. I continued to oversee the women's conference for our church, as well as working with my husband as mission directors.

Over the past couple years, the Lord began to stir in our hearts to plant a church. After much prayer and godly counsel, we made the decision to step out in faith to pioneer a church here in the United States. My husband and I both preach in the church, sometimes as a team and other times individually. I also speak at women's events and Bible studies.

We will continue to build "Hope for Children" orphanages and girls rescue homes overseas, but are also now in the process of planting a life-giving church in the city of Orlando, Florida. It is an honor to be a part of what God is doing and it's exciting to see how He is building His Church!

Q: In what ways have you experienced the "stained glass ceiling" in church life?

SW: I am grateful that my home church was a place where it was common for women to be in ministry. Growing up, my parents showed us a great example of a husband and wife pastoring together as a team. Throughout my life, my mom ministered alongside my dad. She was a worship leader, preached in main services periodically, and led women's Bible studies. Then when my dad went to be with the Lord in 2009, she became the senior pastor. Seeing her rise up in strength during that difficult season was a powerful example in my life.

The only times I have felt "inhibited" in operating in the gifts have been in other settings or nations we have traveled to where women are not valued or received as ministers of the gospel. In those settings, many times my husband would share with the congregation that we are a team and minister together.

YOUR CHALLENGES:

Q: What has been the biggest challenge for you to overcome as a woman in ministry?

SW: When I was a single woman operating in pastoral roles in our church, the biggest challenge I had was when there were male team leaders who had a challenge with following a female leader. Sometimes I felt inadequate, but thankfully during that season I had supervising pastors who were very supportive and encouraged me through the process.

As a married woman with children, the challenge I faced was juggling ministry and raising a family. There were seasons when my children were first born that I had to pull back some, but I never stopped being involved in some way. I had to learn a new rhythm in ministry as I had children. What I have realized is that each season brings different challenges, but the important thing is to keep your eyes on Jesus, trust His timing and find avenues to continue to give out.

One area that I've fought was the tendency to compare myself with other women in ministry. What I am constantly reminded of in the Word is that we are all a vital part of the body of Christ and each person has a unique role, a divine assignment. When I meditate on who God has made me to be, His assignment for my life and the vast need in the world, I am free to fulfill the purpose God has for me!

Q: How would you encourage women who feel called to the ministry but face disapproval and the barrier of a stained glass ceiling?

SW: My encouragement to women is to find a life-giving, Bible-believing church that places value on women and is empowering them to be all God has called them to be.

I think just as women are functioning in other parts of society while raising their children, they can also function within the church in some capacity without neglecting raising their children. Each woman should pray and be led by the Spirit in what is right for them and their family in each season.

Q: Do you think people expect a woman to be more qualified than a man to take on a ministry role?

SW: Sometimes there are expectations from churches and environments that require women to have more seminary or training. The main thing that is important for any person (male or female) is the anointing of God. Joyce Meyer is a great example to all women in ministry because she didn't go through formal seminary training but went through, as she calls it, the "school of the Holy Spirit." Her life experiences, commitment to Bible study and obedience to God opened supernatural doors.

YOUR HUSBAND:

Q: Describe your husband's role in supporting or encouraging you in your calling.

SW: I am thankful that my husband has always been supportive of me in the call of God on my life. He has encouraged me and given me many opportunities to speak or lead.

We definitely feel like we are a "mother and

father" figure to those we are pastoring. There are always challenges with people having opinions or expectations of how we should operate, but as long as we, as a couple, are in agreement that is the main thing.

Q: If you could coach a young husband/pastor in how to encourage/release his wife and her gifts in the church, what would you say to him?

SW: I would encourage him to first identify his wife's gifts, passions and calling through a gift assessment. Then encourage and empower his wife to start operating in areas that she is passionate about. I would also say that there are times when some women need to be challenged or "pushed" to step out past their fears.

In my own life there have been times when my dad (who was also my pastor) would call on me to speak or lead when I didn't always feel capable of doing that, but those experiences helped me to grow. There have also been times when my husband has encouraged me to speak or step out in ways that were uncomfortable. I am grateful for their encouragement, because I was able to help people in a greater way and grew.

You can connect with Sarah at:

www.victoryorlando.com

www.inspireintl.com

Twitter: @sarahwehrli

Instagram: @sarahwehrli

CHAPTER 9

YOUR ASSIGNMENT

Your mission, should you choose to accept it, is to fulfill the will of God in your own life!" Are you ready? Your mission is far more important than the Mr. Phelps line from *Mission Impossible*. Fortunately, your mission is possible and this book won't self-destruct in five seconds!

So, what is your assignment? You've read about my story and the highlighted profiles of numerous women leaders in the church—what about you? Has God called you to the ministry? Leadership in the church? Teaching? Preaching?

What will your life look like after you read this book? Will you embrace your future with faith and confidence? Will you return to the same old, same old? Will you leave the reluctant leader syndrome behind? Will you step up to the leadership plate? Will you spend some time seeking the Lord to get clarification on His calling in your life?

Let's wrap up this book by looking at five practical steps

you can take to walk out your calling as a woman leader in the church.

First, renew your commitment to *live by the Word.*

Second, identify and be confident in your *gifts.*

Third, spend time prayerfully discovering, defining or redefining your *mission.*

Fourth, clarify the *vision* God has given you for fulfilling your purpose.

Fifth, seek *godly counsel.*

Doing these things will reinvigorate your confidence in your calling and you will be well on your way to being more effective and fruitful in your life and ministry.

#1: LIVE BY THE WORD

Perhaps you sense the Lord's call to lead, teach, or preach, but you don't know where to begin. At the end of the day, God's Word is the light for your path. People's opinions can change. Our own hopes and desires can fluctuate. God's Word and His calling don't change. *"For God's gifts and his call can never be withdrawn"* (Romans 11:29, NLT).

His Word gives us understanding. His Word is an anchor for our soul. Jesus discovered His mission, fulfilled His purpose, and quenched the devil's lies and roadblocks with the Word. We are to do the same. He said, *"Man shall not live by bread alone, but by every word that proceeds from the mouth of God"* (Matthew 4:4, NKJV).

We are to live by the Word of God. What words from His Word has the Lord spoken to you over the years? What specific passage(s) of Scripture has God used to call you?

I distinctly remember the impact of these three passages: Romans 10:13-15, John 21:15-17 and Colossians 1:28-29. At strategic times in my early Christian life, God spoke these to my heart and I knew these were my "Calling Scriptures." There has been great confidence and loads of grace to live out the words that have proceed from God's mouth to my heart.

What about you? What scriptures has God spoken to you? Are you living by the words God has given you? Perhaps it would be good to revisit your calling and write down the verses God has spoken to you from His Word:

My Calling Scriptures: _____

#2: IDENTIFY YOUR GIFTS

Have you identified your God-given gifts? What type of gifts have you been given? Most people find their gifts fall under one of two categories: *speaking gifts* or *serving gifts*. God has gifted some people with speaking gifts, while He has gifted others with serving gifts. When you identify which of these two categories you have been primarily gifted in, it will help you to walk out your God-given calling.

1 Peter 4:10-11 makes it simple: *"Each of you should use whatever gift you have received to serve others, as faithful stewards of God's grace in its various forms.* **If anyone speaks, they should do so as one who speaks the very words of God. If anyone serves, they should do so with the strength God provides,** *so that in all things God may be praised through Jesus Christ. To him be the glory and the power for ever and ever. Amen"* (NIV, emphasis mine).

If you love to communicate God's message to people through any or all of the following avenues: preaching, teaching, songwriting or singing, acting, filmmaking, writing or other ways—you likely have speaking gifts. Those with speaking gifts enjoy talking, sharing, being up front, on a stage, leading, communicating, conveying a message, creating videos, writing a blog, script, book or any number of things. Speaking gifts are needed. God uses people with speaking gifts to serve Him in full-time, vocational ministry as well as in part-time or volunteer ministry. Don't shrink from this gift—recognize it and seek the Lord on how to use your gifts in the most effective ways in His church.

If you love to help others experience the gospel in any number of ways whether working behind the scenes, bringing aid, supporting leaders, doing tasks or assisting and lifting the load, that's your cue that you have serving gifts. Those with serving gifts enjoy working outside of the spotlight and they are often good at administrating, coordinating, organizing, preparing, creating, ministering or helping others with whatever needs to happen to get the job done. Serving gifts are needed. God uses people with serving gifts in full-time, vocational ministry as well as in part-time or volunteer ministry. If you have serving gifts, don't minimize these gifts. Seek the Lord on how to use your gifts in the most effective ways in His church.

Of course, all of us are called to speak and serve as we share the gospel and serve one another in love so in some ways, everyone is gifted in both categories. However, when it comes to your specific calling, one of these categories will likely be more dominant, more comfortable and more fulfilling for you. This is the manifold grace of God in operation. Identify your gifts and then use those gifts to minister to others!

Check the one that most fits you. I believe my primary gifts fall under:

__Speaking Gifts   *__Serving Gifts*

#3: DISCOVER YOUR MISSION

What's your mission? Your purpose? Why do you exist? Have you written it down?

Jesus knew His mission. He knew who He was, where He came from, whose He was and where He was going. He consistently used phrases like, "I have come…" and "For this purpose…" Jesus made it clear in John 10:10, *"The thief does not come except to steal, and to kill, and to destroy. I have come that they may have life, and that they may have it more abundantly"* (NKJV).

Jesus knew why He had come. He knew His purpose. He didn't have His own agenda. Jesus made it clear that He only wanted to do the Father's will. *"I am able to do nothing from Myself [independently, of My own accord—but only as I am taught by God and as I get His orders]. Even as I hear, I judge [I decide as I am bidden to decide. As the voice comes to Me, so I give a decision], and My judgment is right (just, righteous), because I do not seek or consult My own will [I have no desire to do what is pleasing to Myself, My own aim, My own purpose] but only the will and pleasure of the Father Who sent Me" (John 5:30, AMP).*

This passage from John 5:30 is a great guide when it comes to discovering your purpose. I remember the day I sat in my car as a fresh Bible School graduate and this passage came alive to my heart like warm honey. I knew if I would align myself with this passage, discovering God's will for my life did not have to be a struggle or a mystery.

There is peace and comfort when we apply this passage to our lives and say like Jesus said: *"I _____ (your name) am able to do nothing from Myself [independently, of My own accord—but only as I am taught by God and as I get His orders]. Even as I hear, I judge [I decide as I am bidden to decide. As the voice comes to Me, so I give a decision], and My judgment is right (just, righteous), because I do not seek or consult My own will [I have no desire to do what is pleasing to Myself, My own aim, My own purpose] but only the will and pleasure of the Father Who sent Me" (John 5:30, AMP, emphasis mine).*

What is the will and pleasure of the Father for your life?

What passions has He put in your heart? What moves you with compassion? What angers you with a righteous indignation? What problem does He want you to solve? Often, these deep desires are indicators of the Father's will and pleasure for our lives—they are our mission.

I have found that God doesn't always show us our mission in one sitting. Often, He gives us pieces to His big puzzle for our lives and over time, the image on the box top comes into focus and we are able to see His mission for us more clearly.

In my own life, I noticed that I am frequently moved with compassion, tears or abundant energy to help people develop a strong foundation built upon Jesus Christ and God's Word in their lives. I get angry when people don't know what they don't know and it causes pain or destruction in their lives. I stay up late and get up early to write things that will establish people in the basics. I am passionate about the basics. When I am helping people get the basics—the foundation stones, the fundamentals, the essentials, the building blocks—on any topic, it thrills my heart. It doesn't matter if I am teaching my kids, explaining something to our staff, preaching to our congregation or writing a book, I always gravitate towards creatively simplifying things and spelling out the steps, processes, systems and puzzle pieces of any given topic—the basics.

So, I have been able to boil down what I believe God's mission is for my ministry into a simple phrase, *"I exist to help people get the basics."* This is my mission.

What's yours? When you boil everything down in your role as a woman, wife, mother and servant of God, why do you exist?

Take some time to complete this sentence.

My Mission:

I exist _____.

#4: CLARIFY YOUR VISION

By definition, vision is what you see. What do you see yourself doing to carry out your mission?

Jesus had a vision to obey His Father. His vision was to do what He saw His Father doing. *"So Jesus answered them by saying, I assure you, most solemnly I tell you, the Son is able to do nothing of Himself (of His own accord); **but He is able to do only what He sees the Father doing**, for whatever the Father does is what the Son does in the same way [in His turn]"* (John 5:19, AMP, emphasis mine).

Jesus fulfilled His mission by carrying out His vision. His vision was to do what He saw the Father doing. Again, He didn't have His own agenda. His vision was God's vision. It's evident that during His earthly ministry, Jesus saw the Father doing three things: teaching, preaching and healing. *"And Jesus went about all Galilee, teaching in their synagogues, preaching the gospel of the kingdom, and healing all kinds of sickness and all kinds of disease among the people"* (Matthew 4:23, NKJV). Jesus' vision to preach, teach, and heal enabled Him to fulfill His mission that we might have life and have it more abundantly.

Jesus saw something even greater than teaching, preaching and healing. Jesus saw you and me. He had a vision to save the world! He saw us and He laid His life down on the cross, *"...for **the joy that was set before Him** endured the cross, despising the shame, and has sat down at the right hand of the throne of God"* (Hebrews 12:2, NKJV, emphasis mine). Jesus lived out His vision and completed His mission!

Jesus told us that the Holy Spirit would show us things to come. *"However, when He, the Spirit of truth, has come, He will guide you into all truth; for He will not speak on His own authority, but whatever He hears He will speak; and He will tell you things to come"* (John 16:13, NKJV).

What has the Holy Spirit shown you? What do you see? What's your vision? Take a moment to complete this sentence:

My Vision:

I see myself doing _____.

#5: SEEK GODLY COUNSEL

Finally, remember you are not alone. Take time to talk with your pastor, your spouse, your parents, mature mentors or trusted Christian leaders to seek their godly counsel and guidance as you move forward in your calling. It often helps to talk to others to get a better and fresh perspective on your life, season, gifts and calling. Their words of wisdom, guidance and affirmation will provide the confirmation and confidence you need to take your place and fulfill God's plan to be the leader He's called you to be.

> *"Where there is no counsel, the people fall; But in the multitude of counselors there is safety" (Proverbs 11:14, NKJV).*

> *I will seek the counsel of these godly people:*

_____

_____

GO YE!

Dear sweet preacher girl, the church needs you and the world is desperate for you to take your place. And, there is a great cloud of witnesses cheering you on from the grandstands of heaven, as well as thousands of men and women here on earth. We need you—with all your dignity and strength—to fulfill your part in the Body of Christ.

> *"She is clothed with strength and dignity, and she laughs without fear of the future. When she speaks, her words are wise, and she gives instructions with kindness."*

> *Proverbs 31:25-26, NLT*

Jesus wants you to step into the calling He has on your life!

> *"You did not choose Me, but I chose you and appointed you that you should go and bear fruit,*

and that your fruit should remain, that whatever you ask the Father in My name He may give you."

John 15:16, NKJV

I hope through reading this book and hearing my story and the featured profiles of other women leaders, you are being strengthened in God's calling on your life. I trust you're hearing the sound of stained glass breaking all around you! I hope we've shattered the myths and empowered you to take your place as a woman called to leadership in the church. Remember, you are living in some of the best days ever for being a woman in ministry. Stay strong in your relationship with the Lord, walk in humility and wisdom and may you, *"...stand perfect and complete in all the will of God" (Colossians 4:12, NKJV).*

Finally, don't ever forget...

"If God is for us, who can be against us?"

Romans 8:31, NKJV

"The Lord announces the word, and the women who proclaim it are a mighty throng..."

Psalm 68:11, NIV

CHAPTER 10

ONE FINAL QUESTION

I'm so glad you've read this book. I have one more thing I want you to share with you. There is a good chance you read this book because you sense God's hand on your life and it's likely you already know Jesus Christ personally, but in the event you do not, let's settle this simple and important question today:

Is your heart right with God?

If not, God has provided a way to make things right—through His Son, Jesus Christ. Our sin—sometimes manifested in apathy towards God or through blatant rebellion—separates us from Him. Jesus came to bridge that great separation between God and us. In order to be the bridge, He had to pay the price our sins demanded—that price was His own death. On the cross, Jesus became sin for us; He took the full punishment and paid the penalty of death sin required. When the price for sin was paid in full, God raised Jesus from death and seated Him at His own right hand. Through Jesus' finished work on the cross, He offers us the free gift of salvation so that we can be reconciled with God. Would you like to be saved and make things right with God today?

Jesus is standing at the door of your heart and if you will surrender your life to Him and confess Him as your Lord, you can receive His forgiveness and get a fresh start in this life and the promise of eternal life in the ages to come. Are you ready to invite Jesus into your life? If so, simply pray this prayer, from your heart:

> *Dear God,*
>
> *I need You in my life. I believe You sent Jesus to this earth to die on a cross for my sins. I do believe He is Lord and You raised Him from the dead. Jesus, I believe You are alive and real. Today, I receive You into my life. At this very moment, I surrender to You and I confess that You are the Lord of my life. Thank You for saving me. I am now a Christian. Help me get to know You better and help me become the person You have created me to be. Amen.*

If you prayed this prayer, I encourage you to do three things:

1.   Start reading the New Testament.

2.   Start talking to Jesus from your heart to His.

3.   Start attending a Spirit-filled Bible church.

Recommended Reading

10 Lies the Church Tells Women
J. Lee Grady

25 Tough Questions About Women and the Church
J. Lee Grady

Beyond Sex Roles
Gilbert Bilezikian

Why Not Women?
Loren Cunningham, David Joel Hamilton and Janice Rogers

Who Said Women Can't Teach?
Charles Trombley

The Woman Question
Kenneth E. Hagin

Daughters of the Church: Women and Ministry From New Testament Times To The Present

Walter L. Liefeld and Ruth A. Tucker

The Role of Women in Ministry

Audio Message by Rick Renner

Getting Women in the Game
Audio Message by Bill Hybels

Putting Women in Their Proper Place – The Role of Women in the Church
Audio Messages by Jeff Jones

APPENDIX

DO THE SCRIPTURES FORBID WOMEN TO PREACH?

The following article was written by Henry Ward Beecher (1813-1887), an American Congregational preacher, orator, and lecturer in the nineteenth century. He was the brother of Harriet Beecher Stowe.[1]

I. There Are Three Views of This Matter

1. That this utterance is official and conclusive. Women are not to speak, however gifted they are.

2. That the authority of the apostle cannot settle the question. Paul forbade women to speak, but he had no business to.

3. That while the Scriptures are of binding authority in matters of faith and morals, this and other injunctions are local, national, and therefore transient.

This latter is the position now to be proved.

II. It Was Not the Design of Christianity to Determine Manners, Customs, Forms of Government, and Ecclesiastical Institutions.

Its aim was to build a new man in Christ Jesus and to this inspired manhood was left the utmost liberty in respect to externals. This view is corroborated by the whole testimony of history. The modern Church is totally different from the assemblies of the first Christians. The civil state has been revolutionized since the time of Christ. The family has changed, and no one organization resembles the organizations of two thousand years ago. The presumption is that when Christ was leaving everything else to the wisdom and experience of after times it did not step in with this single exception and fix the position of women. Such a course would have been contrary to its genius in every other direction.

III. Such a Universal Limitation Could Not Have Taken Place Without Violence to Jewish Ideas.

Woman was far more nearly equal to man among the Hebrews than among other Oriental nations. She was a public instructor. Note the cases of Miriam, Deborah, Hannah, Huldah, Anna, and the prediction of Joel, "Your sons and your daughters shall prophesy," with Peter's comment in Acts 2. So, when the Spirit of God rests upon them and they have a message to give, if you undertake to set up the letter of Paul round about them, I will set up the message which says, "On My handmaidens will I pour out My Spirit, and they shall prophesy." True, in the synagogue it was forbidden for women to teach, but the service was not extemporary, but liturgical and expository; and women had not the technical education for it. But, outside the synagogue, it was eminently in accordance with the Hebrew sentiment that women should speak out—and speak in meetings, too.

IV. Only to Greek Churches Were There Such Limitations to Women's Rights and Privileges.

The text in 1 Timothy 2:11, 12 was addressed not to Jewish, but to Greek assemblies. Why this distinction? Look at the condition of Greek women. The highest thought of womanhood that the Greeks had was that a woman should remain at home, that she should serve her husband and his household, and that she should not be known beyond her own family. She was not permitted to go into the street unless veiled, otherwise her reputation for virtue was destroyed. For a woman to do what is done by women in modern civilized nations, to develop that which the poorest man toils to give his daughters—to learn music, poetry, art, and philosophy—was to stamp her as a courtesan. Such being the popular feeling and custom, what would have been the effect if a Greek had looked in on a Christian meeting and seen a woman rise uncovered and pour out her heart? He would have said, "That is Christianity, is it? Why, then the church is but a house of orgies. I understand your new religion. It teaches our wives that they must forsake their virtue and go out into public exposure and do as courtesans do." Therefore it was that Paul said, "You shall not violate the customs of your country. You shall not bring into discredit the religion of Christ by doing that which can be interpreted but in one direction by every man who sees it. I forbid your women to teach in Greek communities."

V. What, Then, May Be Considered a Fair Interpretation of This?

1.   Is it right to say that this is the last word which the genius of Christianity had for women? Are you to take a command which had a peculiar interpretation in one province of the globe and in no other and make it the criterion for judging of woman's position and instruction everywhere? Shall this be done where Christianity has raised and inspired woman, and shall a manacle, which belonged to the degradation of the Greek period, be put upon the limbs of enfranchised womanhood? You might as well say that the command of the physician to the leper is the prescription that you should take care of your children by.

2.   Scripture commands are binding only where they apply: e.g., we are commanded to "honour the king," but what about countries where there is no king? And you cannot give a rigid interpretation to the text without running against the whole fruit of civilization for the last 1,800 years. Are you going to put back the shadow on the dial? Christianity has made woman a prophetess and no false interpretation of the text can ever close her mouth.

3.   It is fair to apply to this subject the argument of Peter in Acts 11:17. If in the providence of God women are called to preach, if their discourse is accompanied with power from on high and blessed to the salvation of souls, then the Spirit itself bears witness to the right of woman to speak and who are we that we should resist God?

4.   Paul's doctrine in Galatians 3:27-28 is the Christian doctrine for the future. "In Christ there is neither male nor female." Faith, hope, love, learning, eloquence, etc., have no sex. Whoever can bring the kingdom of God nearer to men has the right to do so. We have trumpets enough; let us have some flutes. Women can sing and speak in the secular sphere often to mightier effect than men; why not, then, in the Divine?

STUDY GUIDE
CONVERSATION STARTERS

CHAPTER ONE

1. Do you know any women or young ladies who are called to lead, preach, or teach? What do you know about their story and challenges?

2. Share your story of being a woman in the church—what is your experience in leadership, teaching or preaching?

CHAPTER TWO

1. How does the difference between the "letter of the law" and the "spirit of the law" apply to this topic?

2. Talk about the "gutter ball" phenomenon. Have you, or others you know, ever thrown gutter balls?

CHAPTER THREE

1. Take time to compare these verses and discuss their congruency: 1 Corinthians 14:34 -35 , 1 Timothy 2:11 -15, Acts 2:17 -18 , Acts 21:8, 1 Corinthians 11:5, 14:3-4, 31.

2. Discuss the cultural atmosphere of early New Testament times and their views on women.

CHAPTER FOUR

1. Discuss the various scenarios for women in the church. What do you think about this?

2. How would you describe the different roles of a wife versus those of a woman?

CHAPTER FIVE

1. To whom did Jesus give the Great Commission in Matthew 28:18 -20? How does this relate to women?

2. Discuss Galatians 3:27 -29. What do you think the Lord is trying to tell us?

CHAPTER SIX

1. Who is your favorite preacher girl in the Bible? Why?

2. Discuss the idea that "the proof is in the fruit."

CHAPTER SEVEN

1. Discuss the way Jesus could have set the record straight on this whole controversy.

2. Talk about Mary at the tomb and the woman at the well. What did they do? Did Jesus approve?

CHAPTER EIGHT

1. Describe Satan's worst nightmare.

2. How important is balance and why?

CHAPTER NINE

1. Describe the peace that comes to your heart when you read John 5:19 and John 5:30.

2. Share your calling versus your mission and/or your vision.

CHAPTER TEN

1. Have you received Jesus as Lord? Would you like to?

2. Share a little about your walk and journey with Jesus.

ENDNOTES

CHAPTER TWO

¹ Bob Rodgers, "Setting the Record Straight on David Yonggi Cho," *CharismaNews*, February 25, 2014, http://www.charismanews.com/opinion/42918-setting-the-record-straight-on-david-yonggi-cho.

² Breakfast with David Yonggi Cho and Rick Warren, interciew, *Pastors.com*, 2001.

³ "Who Is Joyce Meyer?" taken from Joyce Meyer Ministries website, accessed May 19, 2014, http://www.joycemeyer.org/AboutUs/FAQ.aspx.

⁴ "Biography," taken from Darlenezschech.com, accessed May 19, 2014, http://www.dalenezschech.com/biography/.

⁵ "Henrietta Mears," taken from the Wheaton College Institute for the Study of American Evangelicals, accessed May 19, 2014, http://www.wheaton.edu/ISAE/Hall-of-Biography/Henrietta-Mears.

⁶ Bill Bright, "Three Women: What a Difference They Made in My Life," Kindling (blog), February 24, 2012. http://inkindle.wordpress.com/2012/02/24/three-women-what-a-difference-they-made-in-my-life-3-by-bill-bright/.

⁷ Happy James, "The Amazon of Literature and Publishing - Henrietta Mears," Soteria (blog), September 23, 2013, http://soteriapublishinghouse.com/?p=3009.

[8] Jo Anne Lyon, "Both Men and Women - An article on 'Spirit-filled Believers'," *The Wesleyan Church.com*, September 30, 2013, http://www.wesleyan.org./227/both-men-and-women-an-article-on-spirit-filled-believers-from-jo-anne-lyon.

[9] Lynne and Bill Hybels, "Evangelicals and Gender Equality," *lynnehybels* (blog), November 18, 2013, http://lynnehybels.blogspot.com/2013/11/evangelicals-and-gender-equality.html

[10] "Aimee Semple McPherson," taken from FourSquare.org, accessed May 19, 2014, http://www.foursquare.org/about/aimee_semple_mcpherson.

[11] Wayne E. Warner, "Maria Woodworth-Etter: A Powerful Voice in the Pentecostal Vangaurd," *Enrichment Journal.ag.org*, http://enrichmentjournal.ag.org/199901/086_woodsworth_etter.cfm

[12] "Purpose," taken from The Kathryn Kuhlman Foundation website, accessed May 19, 2014, http://kathrynkuhlman.com/about.html.

[13] Taken from T.D. Jakes website, accessed June 30, 2014, http://www.tdjakes.org/.

[14] Taken from Hillsong website, accessed June 30, 2014, https://hillsong.com./colour.

[15] Nancy Beach, "Women in Church Leadership-Disappointed But Not Despairing," *Slingshot* (blog), February 20, 2013, http://slingshotgroup.org/women/.

[16] Taken from Mercy Ministries website, accessed July 7, 2014, http://www.mercyministries.org.

CHAPTER THREE

[1] *Vine's Expository Dictionary of Biblical Words*, s.v. "prophesy."

[2] *Thayer's Greek Lexicon*, s.v. "prophesy."

[3] *Adam Clarke Commentary*, note on Acts 2:17, http://www.sacred-texts.com/bib/cmt/clarke/act002.htm.

[4] Ibid

[5] Taken from the Jewish *Talmud*, Mishna sotah 3.4, B sotah 20a.

[6] Origen, *Fragments on 1 Corinthians*, quoted in Tucker and Liefeld, *Daughters of the Church*, 106.

[7] Phelips, *The Churches and Modern Thought*: p203

[8] Martin Luther, quoted in Tucker and Liefeld, *Daughters of the Church*, 174.

[9] *Adam Clarke Commentary*, note on 1 Corinthians 14:34, http://godrules.net/library/clarke/clarke1cor14.htm.

[10] *International Standard Bible Encyclopedia*, s.v. "woman." http://www.internationalstandardbible.com/W/woman/html.

CHAPTER FOUR

[1] J. Lee Grady, 1*0 Lies the Church Tells Women*: How the Bible Has Been Misused to Keep Women in Spiritual Bondage, (Lake Mary, FL: Creation House, 2000), 23.

[2] *New Exhaustive Strong's Numbers and Concordance with Expanded Greek-Hebrew Dictionary*, s.v. "woman" and "man."

[3] *Nelson's Illustrated Bible Dictionary*, s.v. "woman."

CHAPTER FIVE

[1] *Matthew Henry Commentary on the Whole Bible, Volume 5*, note on John chapter 20, http://www.ccel.org/ccel/henry/mhc5.john.xxi.html.

[2] *International Standard Bible Encyclopedia*, s.v. "woman." http://www.internationalstandardbible.com/W/woman.html.

CHAPTER SEVEN

[1] *International Standard Bible Encyclopedia*, s.v. "woman." http://www.internationalstandardbible.com/W/woman.html.

[2] Merrill F. Unger, *The New Unger's Bible Dictionary*, (Chicago: Moody Press 1988), s.v. "Priscil'la."

[3] Kenneth Wuest, *Wuest's Word Studies from the Greek New Testament*, (Grand Rapids: Wm. B. Eerdman's Publishing Co., 1940), 259.

[4] *Vine's Expository Dictionary of Biblical Words*, s.v. "succourer."

[5] *Thayer's Greek Lexicon*, s.v. "succourer."

[6] *International Standard Bible Encyclopedia*, s.v. "woman." http://www.internationalstandardbible.com/W/woman.html.

[7] *Adam Clarke Commentary*, note on Romans 16:12, http://sacred-texts.com/bib/cmt/clarke/rom016.htm.

[8] *Matthew Henry Commentary on the Whole Bible, Volume 6*, note on Romans chapter 16, http://www.ccel.org/ccel/henry/mhc6.Rom.xvii.html.

[9] *Adam Clarke Commentary*, note on Acts 21:9, http://sacred-texts.com/bib/cmt/clarke/act021.htm.

[10] *International Standard Bible Encyclopedia*, s.v. "woman." http://www.internationalstandardbible.com/W/woman.html.

[11] Ibid.

[12] Lucille Sider Dayton and Donald W. Dayton, "Women in the Holiness Movement," Education and Clergy Development of the Wesleyan Church, 2013, p. 4.

[13] Ibid., p. 12-14.

[14] Ibid., p. 19.

[15] Ibid., p. 7.

[16] Ibid., p. 23.

CHAPTER EIGHT

[1] Eliza Collins, "Who talks more: Men or women?" *USAToday,* February 21, 2013, http://www.usatoday.com/story/news/nation/2013/02/21/girls-talk-more/1935963.

APPENDIX

[1] Do the Scriptures Forbid Women from Preaching, taken from Tony Cooke Ministries Website, accessed May 5, 2014, http://www.tonycooke.org/free_resources/articles_others/women_preachers.html

ABOUT THE AUTHOR

BETH JONES

Beth Jones and her husband, Jeff, are the founders and senior pastors of Valley Family Church in Kalamazoo, Michigan, planted in 1991 and named by Outreach magazine as one of the fastest growing churches in America in 2009 and 2010. They also lead Jeff and Beth Jones Ministries, an organization dedicated to helping people *get the basics*. Beth and Jeff have four children and they make their home in the Kalamazoo area.

Beth grew up in Lansing, Michigan, was raised as a Catholic and at the end of her freshman year in college she came into a personal relationship with Christ through the testimony of her roommate. It was there, at age 19, she realized God's plan for her to preach and teach the gospel through writing and speaking. She has been following that call ever since.

Beth is the author of 20 books, including the popular *7 Basics* book and the *Getting a Grip on the Basics* series, which has been translated into over a dozen foreign languages and is being used by thousands of churches around the world. She also writes *The Basics Daily Devo*, a free, daily edevotional for thousands of subscribers.

The heart of Beth's message is a passion to help people *get the basics*! Through down-to-earth teaching, she helps people connect-the-dots and inspires them to follow Jesus and live the successful, fruitful life God desires for them.

Beth attended Boston University in Boston, Massachusetts and received her ministry training at Rhema Bible Training Center in Tulsa, Oklahoma.

For more spiritual growth resources or to connect with Beth, please visit:

www.valleyfamilychurch.org

www.jeffandbethjones.com

www.facebook.com/jeffandbethjones

www.twitter.com/bethjones

www.instagram.com/bethjones

PRAYER OF SALVATION

God loves you—no matter who you are, no matter what your past. God loves you so much that He gave His one and only begotten Son for you. The Bible tells us that "...whoever believes in Him shall not perish but have eternal life" (John 3:16 NIV). Jesus laid down His life and rose again so that we could spend eternity with Him in heaven and experience His absolute best on earth. If you would like to receive Jesus into your life, say the following prayer out loud and mean it from your heart.

Heavenly Father, I come to You admitting that I am a sinner. Right now, I choose to turn away from sin, and I ask You to cleanse me of all unrighteousness. I believe that Your Son, Jesus, died on the cross to take away my sins. I also believe that He rose again from the dead so that I might be forgiven of my sins and made righteous through faith in Him. I call upon the name of Jesus Christ to be the Savior and Lord of my life. Jesus, I choose to follow You and ask that You fill me with the power of the Holy Spirit. I declare that right now I am a child of God. I am free from sin and full of the righteousness of God. I am saved in Jesus' name. Amen.

If you prayed this prayer to receive Jesus Christ as your Savior for the first time, please contact us on the Web at **www.harrisonhouse.com** to receive a free book.

Or you may write to us at
Harrison House • P.O. Box 35035 • Tulsa, Oklahoma 74153